Full-Stack Django Essentials

Essentials

From Database to Deployment; Everything You Need to Know to Build Full-Stack Django Apps

Steve Rankin

Table of Contents

From Database to Deployment; Everything You Need to Know to
Build Full-Stack Django Apps   0

Preface   **5**

Chapter 1: Introduction to Full-Stack Django Development   **7**

1.1 What is Full-Stack Development?   7

1.2 Why Django?   12

1.3 Overview of the Django Ecosystem   18

1.4 Setting Up Your Development Environment   24

1.5 Project Structure and Best Practices   30

Chapter 2: Django Fundamentals   **36**

2.1 Understanding the MTV (Model-Template-View) Architecture   36

2.2 Creating Your First Django Project and App   41

2.3 Working with Settings and URLs   45

2.4 Basic Views and Template Rendering   51

2.5 Introduction to Django's Command-Line Interface (manage.py)   55

Chapter 3: Database Essentials with Django Models   **60**

3.1 Introduction to Databases and ORMs   60

3.2 Defining Models and Fields   65

3.3 Database Migrations (Making Changes to Your Database)   68

3.4 Working with the Django Admin Interface   73

3.5 Querying the Database with the Django ORM   77

Chapter 4: Advanced Model Techniques   **83**

4.1 Model Relationships (One-to-One, One-to-Many, Many-to-Many)
83

4.2 Model Inheritance   88

4.3 Custom Model Methods and Properties   92

4.4 Using Managers and QuerySets Effectively   97

4.5 Advanced Database Queries and Aggregations   102

Chapter 5: Views and URL Routing   **108**

5.1 Function-Based Views vs. Class-Based Views   108

5.2 URL Patterns and Regular Expressions   113

5.3 Handling HTTP Requests (GET, POST, PUT, DELETE)   118

5.4 Form Handling and Validation   125

5.5 Working with Sessions and Cookies   134

Chapter 6: Django REST Framework (DRF)   **140**

    6.1 Introduction to RESTful APIs   140

    6.2 Setting Up DRF   145

    6.3 Serializers and Deserializers   149

    6.4 ViewSets and Routers   154

    6.5 Authentication and Permissions in DRF   160

    6.6 API Documentation using Swagger or Redoc   167

Chapter 7: Django Templates and Static Files   **173**

    7.1 Template Syntax and Variables   173

    7.2 Template Inheritance and Inclusion   178

    7.3 Working with Static Files (CSS, JavaScript, Images)   184

    7.4 Template Filters and Tags   190

    7.5 Building Dynamic HTML with Django Templates   197

Chapter 8: Frontend Integration with JavaScript   **204**

    8.1 Integrating JavaScript with Django Templates   204

    8.2 Using AJAX to Fetch Data from the Backend   211

    8.3 Working with Frontend Frameworks (e.g., integrating Vue.js or React with Django) (optional)   218

    8.4 Using Web Sockets with Django Channels   225

Chapter 9: Forms and User Interfaces   **233**

    9.1 Building Complex Forms with Django Forms   233

    9.2 Customizing Form Rendering   238

    9.3 Implementing User Authentication and Authorization   245

    9.4 Creating User-Friendly Interfaces with HTML and CSS   252

Chapter 10: Testing Your Django Application   **261**

    10.1 Writing Unit Tests and Integration Tests   261

    10.2 Using Django's Testing Tools   266

    10.3 Test-Driven Development (TDD)   273

    10.4 Debugging and Troubleshooting   279

Chapter 11: Deployment Strategies   **287**

    11.1 Preparing Your Application for Deployment   287

    11.2 Choosing a Hosting Platform   293

    11.3 Setting Up a Production Database (PostgreSQL, MySQL)   298

    11.4 Configuring a Web Server (Nginx, Apache)   304

    11.5 Deploying with Docker and Containerization (Optional)   311

11.6 Using CI/CD Pipelines 318

Chapter 12: Performance Optimization and Security **324**

12.1 Caching Strategies 324

12.2 Database Optimization 333

12.3 Security Best Practices (CSRF, XSS, SQL Injection Prevention) 339

12.4 Monitoring and Logging 345

12.5 Scalability Considerations 352

Conclusion **358**

Appendix A: Django Resources and Further Learning **361**

Appendix B: Example Project Walkthrough **366**

Preface

Welcome to "Full-Stack Django Essentials," your comprehensive guide to mastering the art of building complete, dynamic web applications with the powerful Django framework. Whether you're a budding developer eager to dive into full-stack development or an experienced programmer looking to streamline your workflow with Django, this book is designed to equip you with the knowledge and practical skills needed to succeed.

In today's fast-paced digital landscape, the ability to create robust, scalable, and feature-rich web applications is more valuable than ever. Django, with its "batteries-included" philosophy, provides a solid foundation for rapid development, enabling you to focus on building your application's unique features rather than reinventing the wheel. From handling complex database interactions to crafting elegant user interfaces and deploying your creations to the cloud, Django simplifies the entire development lifecycle.

This book takes you on a journey from the fundamental concepts of Django's Model-Template-View (MTV) architecture to the intricacies of building RESTful APIs with Django REST Framework, and finally, to the crucial stages of testing, deployment, and optimization. We emphasize practical, hands-on learning, providing clear, concise explanations and real-world examples that you can adapt to your own projects.

We understand that full-stack development can seem daunting, with its myriad of technologies and best practices. That's why we've structured this book to provide a logical, step-by-step progression, building your understanding incrementally. By the end of this book, you'll not only have a deep understanding of Django but also the confidence to tackle real-world web development challenges.

This book is more than just a collection of tutorials; it's a roadmap to becoming a proficient Django developer. We encourage you to experiment, explore, and most importantly, build. The world of web development is constantly evolving, and Django provides a robust and flexible platform to keep pace.

We hope this book inspires you to create amazing web applications and empowers you to bring your ideas to life. Let's embark on this exciting journey together.

Chapter 1: Introduction to Full-Stack Django Development

Welcome to the exciting world of full-stack web development with Django. In this chapter, we're going to lay the groundwork, understanding what full-stack actually means, why Django is such a fantastic choice, and how to get your environment set up. So, grab your favorite beverage, and let's dive in!

1.1 What is Full-Stack Development?

So, you've heard the term "full-stack developer" thrown around, but what does it *actually* mean? Let's break it down. Essentially, a full-stack developer is a jack-of-all-trades in the web development world, capable of handling both the front-end (client-side) and back-end (server-side) aspects of an application.[1]

Think of it like building a restaurant. The front-end is the dining area, the menu design, and how customers interact with the staff.[2] The back-end is the kitchen, the inventory management, and the systems that keep everything running smoothly. A full-stack developer is someone who can design the dining area *and* manage the kitchen.[3]

In the context of web development, this translates to:

- **Front-End Development:**
    - This is what users see and interact with in their browsers.[4]

- It involves technologies like HTML (structure), CSS (styling), and JavaScript (interactivity).[5]
- Front-end developers focus on user experience (UX) and user interface (UI) design.[6]
- They might use frameworks like React, Vue.js, or Angular to build complex interfaces.[7]
- **Back-End Development:**
  - This is the server-side logic that powers the application.[8]
  - It involves handling data, processing requests, and managing databases.[9]
  - Technologies include server-side languages like Python, Node.js, Ruby, and databases like PostgreSQL, MySQL, or MongoDB.
  - Back-end developers focus on performance, security, and scalability.
- **Database Management:**
  - Full-stack developers often work with databases to store and retrieve data.[10]
  - Understanding database design, queries, and optimization is crucial.[11]
- **Server Management:**
  - They may also handle server configuration and deployment.[12]
  - This involves tasks like setting up web servers (Nginx, Apache) and managing cloud services.[13]

Why is Full-Stack Development Important?

- **Versatility:** Full-stack developers can handle multiple aspects of a project, reducing the need for large teams.[14]

- **Faster Development:** They can quickly prototype and iterate on ideas.[15]
- **Better Understanding:** They have a holistic view of the application, leading to better decision-making.[16]
- **Cost-Effective:** Smaller companies or startups can rely on full-stack developers to handle various tasks.[17]

Practical Implementation: A Simple Example

Let's create a very basic example to illustrate the concept. We'll build a simple web page that displays a message retrieved from a Python back-end.

1. Back-End (Python):

First, we'll create a simple Python script that returns a message:

Python

simple_backend.py

from http.server import BaseHTTPRequestHandler, HTTPServer

class SimpleHandler(BaseHTTPRequestHandler):

  def do_GET(self):

    self.send_response(200)

    self.send_header('Content-type', 'text/html')

    self.end_headers()

```python
        message = "Hello from the Python back-end!"

        self.wfile.write(message.encode())

def run(server_class=HTTPServer, handler_class=SimpleHandler, port=8000):

    server_address = ('', port)

    httpd = server_class(server_address, handler_class)

    print(f'Starting server on port {port}')

    httpd.serve_forever()

if __name__ == "__main__":

    run()
```

- This code sets up a basic HTTP server using Python's http.server module.
- When a get request is made, it returns "Hello from the Python back-end!"

To run this, save it as simple_backend.py and run it from your terminal:

Bash

```bash
python simple_backend.py
```

2. Front-End (HTML/JavaScript):

Now, let's create an HTML file that fetches the message from the Python server:

HTML

```html
<!DOCTYPE html>

<html>

<head>

  <title>Full-Stack Example</title>

</head>

<body>

  <div id="message"></div>

  <script>

  fetch('http://localhost:8000')

  .then(response => response.text())

  .then(data => {

  document.getElementById('message').textContent = data;

  });

  </script>

</body>

</html>
```

- This HTML file uses JavaScript's fetch API to make a GET request to http://localhost:8000, the address of our Python server.
- It then displays the received message in the div with the ID "message".

Save this as index.html and open it in your browser.

Explanation:

- The Python script acts as the back-end, handling requests and providing data.
- The HTML and JavaScript act as the front-end, displaying the data to the user.[18]
- This very basic example shows how the front and back end work together.

This example, while simple, illustrates the core concept of full-stack development: both the front-end and back-end work together to create a functional web application.[19]

1.2 Why Django?

So, you're wondering, "Why Django? There are so many frameworks out there!" That's a valid question. Let's break down the key reasons why Django stands out from the crowd.

1. "Batteries Included" Philosophy:

Django is famous for its "batteries included" approach.[2] This means it comes with a lot of built-in features that you'd typically need to build a web application. Think of it as a Swiss Army knife for web development.

- **ORM (Object-Relational Mapper):** This lets you interact with databases using Python code, eliminating the need to write raw SQL.[3]
- **Admin Interface:** Django automatically generates a powerful admin interface for managing your data.[4]
- **Templating Engine:** Django's templating system makes it easy to generate dynamic HTML.[5]
- **Authentication and Authorization:** Built-in tools for handling user accounts and permissions.[6]

This means you spend less time setting up basic functionality and more time building your application's unique features.

2. Python Power:

Django is built on Python, a language known for its readability and simplicity.[7] Python's clean syntax makes it easy to learn and write code, especially if you're new to web development.[8] Plus, Python has a massive ecosystem of libraries and tools that you can leverage in your Django projects.[9]

3. Security:

Django takes security seriously. It helps protect your application from common vulnerabilities like:

- **SQL Injection:** Django's ORM helps prevent this by automatically escaping user inputs.
- **Cross-Site Scripting (XSS):** Django's templating engine helps prevent XSS attacks.[10]
- **Cross-Site Request Forgery (CSRF):** Django provides built-in CSRF protection.[11]

This built-in security gives you a strong foundation to build secure web applications.

4. Community and Ecosystem:

Django has a large and active community.[12] This means you'll find plenty of resources, tutorials, and support when you need it. Plus, there's a vast ecosystem of third-party packages that extend Django's functionality.

5. Rapid Development:

Django's design philosophy emphasizes rapid development.[13] Its "don't repeat yourself" (DRY) principle and high-level abstractions allow you to build and deploy applications quickly.[14]

Practical Implementation: Creating a Basic Django Project

Let's see Django's rapid development in action by creating a simple Django project.

Step 1: Install Django (if you haven't already):

Bash

pip install Django

Step 2: Create a Django Project:

Bash

django-admin startproject myproject

This creates a directory named myproject with the initial project structure.

Step 3: Navigate to the Project Directory:

Bash

cd myproject

Step 4: Create a Django App:

Bash

python manage.py startapp myapp

This creates a directory named myapp within your project. Apps are modular components of your Django project.[15]

Step 5: Define a Simple View:

Open myapp/views.py and add the following code:

Python

from django.http import HttpResponse

def hello(request):

return HttpResponse("Hello, Django!")

This defines a simple view that returns a "Hello, Django!" message.

Step 6: Define a URL Pattern:

Open myproject/urls.py and add the following code:

Python

from django.contrib import admin

from django.urls import path

from myapp import views

urlpatterns = [

  path('admin/', admin.site.urls),

  path('hello/', views.hello, name='hello'),

]

This maps the URL /hello/ to the hello view we created.

Step 7: Run the Development Server:

Bash

python manage.py runserver

Open your browser and navigate to http://127.0.0.1:8000/hello/. You should see "Hello, Django!" displayed in your browser.

Explanation:

- We created a project and an app with just a few commands.
- We defined a view and a URL pattern to display a simple message.
- We ran the development server and saw our application in action.

This simple example demonstrates Django's rapid development capabilities. With just a few lines of code, we created a functional web page.

In essence, Django simplifies and accelerates the web development process, allowing you to focus on building the unique features of your applications.[16]

1.3 Overview of the Django Ecosystem

When you start working with Django, you'll encounter a set of core components that work together to build web applications. It's like a well-organized toolkit, where each tool has a specific purpose. Let's take a closer look.

Models: Defining Your Data

At the heart of any web application is data. Django's Models are where you define the structure of your data. Think of them as blueprints for your database tables. They allow you to define what data you want to store and how it relates to other pieces of data.

Here's a basic example: Let's say we're building a blog. We might have a Post model that looks like this:

Python

```python
# myapp/models.py
from django.db import models
class Post(models.Model):
    title = models.CharField(max_length=200)
    content = models.TextField()
    pub_date = models.DateTimeField('date published')
    def __str__(self):
    return self.title
```

In this code:

- We're creating a Post model with three fields: title, content, and pub_date.

- **CharField** is used for short text, **TextField** for longer text, and **DateTimeField** for dates and times.
- The __str__ method tells Django how to represent a **Post** object as a string.

Django's ORM (Object-Relational Mapper) then translates these models into database tables. So, you don't have to write raw SQL queries; Django handles that for you.

Views: Handling Requests and Responses

Views are where the logic of your application lives. They receive HTTP requests from users and return HTTP responses. Think of them as the conductors of your web application, orchestrating the flow of data.

Here's a simple view that displays a list of posts:

Python

```
# myapp/views.py
from django.shortcuts import render
from .models import Post
def post_list(request):
    posts = Post.objects.all()
        return render(request, 'myapp/post_list.html', {'posts':
posts})
```

In this code:

- We're fetching all **Post** objects from the database using **Post.objects.all()**.
- We're using **render** to pass the posts to a template called **myapp/post_list.html**.

Views can handle various HTTP methods like GET, POST, PUT, and DELETE, allowing you to build complex interactions.

Templates: Presenting Data to Users

Templates are HTML files that define the structure and presentation of your web pages. They allow you to dynamically generate HTML by embedding variables and logic.

Here's an example of a template that displays the list of posts:

HTML

```
<!DOCTYPE html>
<html>
<head>
<title>Post List</title>
</head>
<body>
  <h1>Posts</h1>
  <ul>
  {% for post in posts %}
  <li>{{ post.title }} - {{ post.pub_date }}</li>
  {% endfor %}
  </ul>
</body>
</html>
```

In this code:

- We're using Django's template language to loop through the posts variable and display their titles and publication dates.

Templates allow you to separate the presentation layer from the application logic, making your code more maintainable.

URLs: Mapping URLs to Views

URLs are the addresses of your web pages. Django's URL patterns define how URLs map to views. Think of them as the routing system of your application.

Here's an example of a URL pattern that maps the /posts/ URL to the post_list view:

Python

```
# myproject/urls.py
from django.contrib import admin
from django.urls import path
from myapp import views
urlpatterns = [
    path('admin/', admin.site.urls),
    path('posts/', views.post_list, name='post_list'),
]
```

In this code:

- We're using path to define a URL pattern.
- The first argument is the URL pattern, and the second argument is the view function.

URLs allow you to create clean and user-friendly URLs for your web application.

Admin Interface: Managing Your Data

Django's admin interface is a powerful tool for managing your data. It automatically generates a user interface for your models, allowing you to create, read, update, and delete data.

To use the admin interface, you need to register your models:

Python

```python
# myapp/admin.py
from django.contrib import admin
from .models import Post
admin.site.register(Post)
```

Then, you can access the admin interface at /admin/ and manage your posts. This feature saves a lot of development time.

Django REST Framework (DRF): Building APIs

Django REST Framework (DRF) is a powerful toolkit for building Web APIs. It allows you to expose your data as JSON or XML, making it accessible to other applications.

Here's an example of a simple API view using DRF:

Python

```python
# myapp/views.py
from rest_framework import serializers, viewsets
```

```python
from .models import Post

class PostSerializer(serializers.ModelSerializer):
    class Meta:
        model = Post
        fields = ('id', 'title', 'content', 'pub_date')

class PostViewSet(viewsets.ModelViewSet):
    queryset = Post.objects.all()
    serializer_class = PostSerializer
```

In this code:

- We're creating a serializer to convert Post objects to JSON.
- We're creating a viewset to handle API requests.

DRF simplifies the process of building RESTful APIs, which are essential for modern web applications.

Django Channels: Real-Time Functionality

Django Channels extends Django to handle WebSockets, allowing you to build real-time applications. Think of chat applications or live dashboards.

Here's a basic example of a WebSocket consumer:

Python

```python
# myapp/consumers.py
import json
from             channels.generic.websocket             import
WebsocketConsumer
```

```python
class ChatConsumer(WebsocketConsumer):
    def connect(self):
    self.accept()

    def disconnect(self, close_code):
    pass
    def receive(self, text_data):
        text_data_json = json.loads(text_data)
        message = text_data_json['message']
        self.send(text_data=json.dumps({
        'message': message
        }))
```

This code sets up a simple echo server. Django channels handles the asynchronus nature of web sockets.

These components work together to form the Django ecosystem, providing a comprehensive toolkit for building web applications. By understanding each component and how they interact, you can leverage Django's power to create robust and scalable web applications.

1.4 Setting Up Your Development Environment

Before we start coding, we need to make sure our workspace is ready. This involves installing Python, setting up a virtual environment, and choosing a good IDE.

1. Installing Python

Django is a Python framework, so you'll need Python installed on your system. If you don't have it already, here's how to get it:

- **Download:** Go to python.org and download the latest stable version of Python.
- **Installation:** Run the installer. Make sure to check the box that says "Add Python to PATH" during installation. This allows you to run Python from your command line.
- **Verification:** Open your terminal or command prompt and type:

Bash

```
python --version
```

or if that does not work, try

Bash

```
python3 --version
```

You should see the Python version number displayed. If you do, you're good to go!

2. Virtual Environments

Virtual environments are essential for managing project dependencies. They create isolated environments for each of your projects, preventing conflicts between different libraries.

Here's how to set up a virtual environment:

- **Create a Virtual Environment:** Open your terminal or command prompt and navigate to the directory where you want to create[1] your project. Then, run:

Bash

python -m venv venv

or if that does not work, try

Bash

python3 -m venv venv

This creates a directory named venv (or whatever name you choose) that contains your virtual environment.

- **Activate the Virtual Environment:**
  - On macOS/Linux:

Bash

source venv/bin/activate

* On Windows:

Bash

venv\Scripts\activate

Once activated, you'll see the name of your virtual environment in your terminal prompt, indicating that it's active.

- **Installing Django:** Now that your virtual environment is active, you can install Django:

Bash

pip install Django

- **Verify Django Installation:**

Bash

django-admin --version

This should display the Django version number.

3. Choosing an IDE (Integrated Development Environment)

While you can use any text editor, an IDE provides features that make development much easier. Here are a few popular choices:

- **VS Code (Visual Studio Code):**
  - A free, open-source IDE from Microsoft.
  - Highly customizable with extensions.
  - Excellent Python support.
  - Built-in terminal and debugging tools.
- **PyCharm:**
  - A dedicated Python IDE from JetBrains.

- Offers advanced features like code completion, refactoring, and debugging.
  - Comes in a free Community Edition and a paid Professional Edition.
- **Sublime Text:**
  - A lightweight and fast text editor.
  - Highly customizable with plugins.
  - Good Python support.

For our examples, we'll be using VS Code, but feel free to use whichever IDE you prefer.

Practical Implementation: Setting Up a Project Directory and Virtual Environment

Let's walk through the steps to set up a project directory and virtual environment:

1. **Create a Project Directory:**

Bash

```
mkdir my_django_project
cd my_django_project
```

2. **Create a Virtual Environment:**

Bash

```
python -m venv venv
```

3. **Activate the Virtual Environment:**

Bash

```
source venv/bin/activate # For macOS/Linux
venv\Scripts\activate # For windows.
```

4. **Install Django:**

Bash

```
pip install Django
```

5. **Verify Installation:**

Bash

```
django-admin --version
```

Now, your environment is all set up, and you're ready to start building Django applications.

Real-World Example:

Imagine you're working on a team with multiple projects. Using virtual environments ensures that each project has its own set of dependencies, preventing conflicts and making it easier to manage your projects.

By setting up your development environment correctly, you're laying a solid foundation for your Django journey. It makes it easier to manage dependencies, write code, and debug issues.

1.5 Project Structure and Best Practices

When you create a new Django project, it comes with a predefined directory structure. Understanding this structure helps you navigate and organize your code effectively. Let's break it down.

Understanding the Default Project Structure

When you run django-admin startproject myproject, Django creates a directory with the following structure:

myproject/
  manage.py
  myproject/
    __init__.py
    asgi.py
    settings.py
    urls.py
    wsgi.py

Let's look at each of these files and directories:

- manage.py: This is a command-line utility that allows you to interact with your Django project. You'll use it for tasks like running the development server, creating database migrations, and running tests.
- myproject/ **(Inner Directory)**: This directory contains the Python packages for your project.
    - __init__.py: An empty file that tells Python that this directory should be considered a Python package.

- asgi.py:[1] An entry-point for ASGI-compatible web servers to serve your project. ASGI (Asynchronous Server Gateway Interface) is used for asynchronous web applications.
- settings.py: This file contains all the settings and configurations for your Django project. It's where you define database connections, installed apps, middleware, and other project-wide settings.
- urls.py: This file defines the URL patterns for your project. It maps URLs to views, which handle the logic of your application.
- wsgi.py: An entry-point for WSGI-compatible web servers to serve your project. WSGI (Web Server Gateway Interface) is the standard interface between web servers and Python web applications.

Creating Apps

In Django, an "app" is a self-contained component that performs a specific function within your project. To create an app, you use the manage.py startapp command. For example:

Bash

python manage.py startapp blog

This creates a directory named blog with the following structure:

blog/

```
__init__.py
admin.py
apps.py
migrations/
    __init__.py
models.py
tests.py
views.py
```

- **models.py**: This file defines the data models for your app.
- **views.py**: This file contains the views that handle the logic of your app.
- **urls.py**: You can create a urls.py inside an app directory to define the url patterns specific to that app.
- **admin.py**: This file allows you to customize the admin interface for your app's models.
- **tests.py**: This file contains the unit tests for your app.
- **migrations/**: This directory contains the database migrations for your app.

Best Practices for Project Structure

Here are some best practices to keep your Django projects organized:

- **Use Apps for Modularization:** Break your project into logical apps. For example, if you're building an e-commerce site, you might have apps for products, orders, and users.
- **Keep Settings Separate:** Use separate settings files for different environments (development, production). You

can use environment variables or multiple settings files to manage this.

- **Use a** requirements.txt **File:** Create a requirements.txt file to list all the dependencies of your project. This makes it easy to set up your project on other machines.

Bash

pip freeze > requirements.txt

- And to install the requirements:

Bash

pip install -r requirements.txt

- **Use Virtual Environments:** Always use virtual environments to isolate your project's dependencies.
- **Follow Django's Conventions:** Stick to Django's naming conventions and file structure. This makes your code more readable and maintainable.
- **Use Version Control:** Use Git to track changes to your code. This allows you to collaborate with others and revert to previous versions if needed.
- **Create App Specific URL files:** create a urls.py file inside of your app directory. Then in the main project urls.py include the app's urls.py file. This helps with modularization of url patterns.

Example app urls.py:

Python

```python
# blog/urls.py
from django.urls import path
from . import views
urlpatterns = [
    path('', views.blog_index, name='blog_index')
]
```

- Example main project urls.py:

Python

```python
# myproject/urls.py
from django.contrib import admin
from django.urls import path, include
urlpatterns = [
    path('admin/', admin.site.urls),
    path('blog/', include('blog.urls'))
]
```

- **Create a** static **Folder:** Place all your static files (CSS, JavaScript, images) in a static folder within your app.

```
blog/
static/
blog/
```

```
css/
js/
images/
```

- **Create a templates Folder:** Place all your templates in a templates folder within your app.

```
blog/
templates/
blog/
index.html
detail.html
```

Real-World Example:

Imagine you're building a large web application with multiple features. By breaking your project into apps, you can assign different teams to work on different features independently. This makes development more efficient and reduces the risk of conflicts.

By following these best practices, you can create well-structured and maintainable Django projects that are easy to work with and scale.

Chapter 2: Django Fundamentals

Let's start building with Django! In this chapter, we'll cover the core concepts that form the foundation of Django development. We're going to understand the MTV architecture, create our first project and app, and learn how to work with settings, URLs, views, and templates. Get ready to build your Django skills!

2.1 Understanding the MTV (Model-Template-View) Architecture

Django uses the Model-Template-View (MTV) architectural pattern. While it shares similarities with the more commonly known Model-View-Controller (MVC) pattern, there are key differences that make Django's approach unique. Understanding these differences is crucial for effective Django development.

Breaking Down the Components

Essentially, MTV separates the concerns of data, presentation, and logic into distinct components. Let's look at each:

- **Model (M):**
    - The Model is your data layer. It defines the structure of your data and handles database interactions.
    - In Django, models are Python classes that inherit from django.db.models.Model. Each class represents a database table, and each attribute represents a table column.

- Django's ORM (Object-Relational Mapper) allows you to interact with the database using Python code, abstracting away the complexities of raw SQL.
- This separation keeps your data logic clean and organized, making it easier to manage and maintain.

Practical Example:

Python

```python
# myapp/models.py
from django.db import models
class Product(models.Model):
    name = models.CharField(max_length=200)
    description = models.TextField()
    price = models.DecimalField(max_digits=10, decimal_places=2)
    stock = models.IntegerField()
    def __str__(self):
        return self.name
```

In this example, we've defined a **Product** model with fields for name, description, price, and stock. Django will translate this into a database table.

- **Template (T):**

- The Template is your presentation layer. It defines how data is displayed to the user.
- Django's template engine allows you to create dynamic HTML pages by embedding variables and logic within your HTML.
- This separation keeps your presentation logic separate from your application logic, making it easier to design and maintain your user interface.

Practical Example:

```
<!DOCTYPE html>

<html>

<head>

<title>{{ product.name }}</title>

</head>

<body>

<h1>{{ product.name }}</h1>

<p>{{ product.description }}</p>

<p>Price: ${{ product.price1 }}</p>

<p>Stock: {{ product.stock }}</p>

</body>
```

```
</html>
```

```
```

This template displays the details of a product, using variables passed from the view.

- **View (V):**
  - The View is your application logic layer. It handles the processing of HTTP requests and returns HTTP responses.
  - Views act as the intermediary between the Model and the Template, retrieving data from the Model and passing it to the Template for rendering.
  - Views can be function-based or class-based, depending on the complexity of the logic.
  - **Practical Example:**

Python

```python
# myapp/views.py
from django.shortcuts import render, get_object_or_404
from .models import Product
def product_detail(request, product_id):
    product = get_object_or_404(Product, pk=product_id)
        return render(request, 'myapp/product_detail.html',
{'product': product})
```

This view retrieves a Product object from the database and passes it to the product_detail.html template.

The "Controller" (URLs)

In Django, the "controller" role is handled by the URL configuration. The urls.py file maps URLs to views, determining which view handles a particular request. This separation of URL routing from view logic keeps your code organized and maintainable.

How MTV Works Together

1. **User Request:** A user makes a request to your web application by entering a URL in their browser.
2. **URL Routing:** Django's URL configuration maps the URL to a specific view.
3. **View Processing:** The view processes the request, retrieves data from the Model (if needed), and prepares the data for presentation.
4. **Template Rendering:** The view passes the data to the Template, which renders the HTML page.
5. **HTTP Response:** Django sends the rendered HTML as an HTTP response to the user's browser.

Real-World Example

Consider an e-commerce website. When a user views a product page:

- The URL /products/123/ is mapped to the product_detail view.
- The product_detail view retrieves the product with ID 123 from the Product model.
- The view passes the product data to the product_detail.html template.

- The template renders the product details, and Django sends the HTML to the user's browser.

This separation of concerns makes Django applications easier to develop, maintain, and scale.

2.2 Creating Your First Django Project and App

We're going to build a simple web application. Before we can start, we need to set up a Django project and an app within that project. Think of a Django project as the overall container for your web application, and an app as a specific feature or module within that container.

Creating a Django Project

First, ensure you have Django installed. If not, open your terminal or command prompt and run:

Bash

pip install Django

Now, let's create a new Django project. Navigate to the directory where you want to store your project and run the following command:[1]

Bash

django-admin startproject myfirstproject

Replace myfirstproject with the name you want for your project. This command creates a directory named myfirstproject with the initial project structure.

Let's explore the directory structure:

```
myfirstproject/
  manage.py
  myfirstproject/
    __init__.py
    asgi.py
    settings.py
    urls.py
    wsgi.py
```

- **manage.py**: This is a command-line utility that allows you to interact with your Django project. You'll use it for tasks like running the development server, creating apps, and managing databases.
- **myfirstproject/ (Inner Directory)**: This directory contains the Python packages for your project.
  - __init__.py: An empty file that tells Python that this directory should be considered a Python package.
  - asgi.py[2] and wsgi.py: These files are entry points for ASGI and WSGI-compatible web servers to serve your project.
  - settings.py: This file contains all the settings and configurations for your Django project.
  - urls.py: This file defines the URL patterns for your project.

Creating a Django App

Now that we have a project, let's create an app within it. Navigate to the myfirstproject directory (the one containing manage.py) and run the following command:

Bash

python manage.py startapp myfirstapp

Replace myfirstapp with the name you want for your app. This command creates a directory named myfirstapp with the initial app structure.

Let's explore the directory structure:

```
myfirstapp/
    __init__.py
    admin.py
    apps.py
    migrations/
        __init__.py
    models.py
    tests.py
    views.py
```

- models.py: This file defines the data models for your app.
- views.py: This file contains the views that handle the logic of your app.
- admin.py: This file allows you to customize the admin interface for your app's models.
- tests.py: This file contains the unit tests for your app.

- migrations/: This directory contains the database migrations for your app.

Registering the App

Before we can use our app, we need to register it in the settings.py file. Open myfirstproject/settings.py and add myfirstapp to the INSTALLED_APPS list:

Python

```python
INSTALLED_APPS = [
    'myfirstapp',
    'django.contrib.admin',
    'django.contrib.auth',
    'django.contrib.contenttypes',
    'django.contrib.sessions',
    'django.contrib.messages',
    'django.contrib.staticfiles',
]
```

This[3] tells Django that our app is part of the project.

Running the Development Server

Now, let's run the development server to see our project in action. In your terminal, navigate to the myfirstproject directory (the one containing manage.py) and run the following command:

Bash

```bash
python manage.py runserver
```

This starts the development server, which you can access by opening your browser and navigating to http://127.0.0.1:8000/. You should see the default Django welcome page.

Example:

Imagine you're building a social media platform. You might create a Django project named socialmedia and apps named users, posts, and messages. Each app would handle a specific feature of the platform.

By creating projects and apps, you can organize your code into manageable modules, making your Django applications easier to develop and maintain.

2.3 Working with Settings and URLs

First, let's get comfortable with the project settings. The settings.py file is the central configuration hub for your Django project. It's where you define everything from database connections to installed apps. Then we will move on to Urls, which are the way your users navigate through your web application.

Understanding Settings

The settings.py file contains a Python module with various variables that control your Django project's behavior. When you create a new project, Django generates a default settings.py file with some essential settings already configured.

Let's examine some key settings:

- **DEBUG**:
  - This setting controls whether Django runs in debug mode. In development, you'll typically set DEBUG = True, which provides detailed error messages and debugging information.
  - In production, you should set DEBUG = False for security and performance reasons.
- **ALLOWED_HOSTS**:
  - This setting specifies the allowed hostnames for your Django application. It's crucial for security, preventing HTTP Host header attacks.
  - In development, you can set ALLOWED_HOSTS = ['*'] or ALLOWED_HOSTS = ['127.0.0.1', 'localhost']. In production, you should specify the actual domain names.
- **INSTALLED_APPS**:
  - This setting lists the apps that are part of your Django project. Each app is a Python package that contributes to your project's functionality.
  - You'll need to add your custom apps to this list.
- **MIDDLEWARE**:
  - This setting lists the middleware classes that Django uses to process requests and responses. Middleware can perform tasks like session management, authentication, and security checks.
- **ROOT_URLCONF**:

- This setting specifies the root URL configuration for your project. By default, it points to myproject.urls, where myproject is the name of your project.
- DATABASES:
  - This setting configures your database connection. Django supports various databases, including SQLite, PostgreSQL, MySQL, and Oracle.
- STATIC_URL:
  - This setting defines the base URL for serving static files, such as CSS, JavaScript, and images.

Practical Implementation: Modifying Settings

Let's modify some settings in our project.

1. Open myproject/settings.py.
2. Change the TIME_ZONE setting to your local time zone. For example:

Python

```
TIME_ZONE = 'Africa/Lagos'
```

3. If you want to use a different database, modify the DATABASES setting. For example, to use PostgreSQL:

Python

```
DATABASES = {
   'default': {
```

```
    'ENGINE': 'django.db.backends.postgresql',
    'NAME': 'mydatabase',
    'USER': 'myuser',
    'PASSWORD': 'mypassword',
    'HOST': '127.0.0.1',
    'PORT': '5432',
    }
}
```

Working with URLs

URLs are the addresses of your web pages. Django uses URL patterns to map URLs to views, which handle the logic for those pages. The urls.py file defines these URL patterns.

Django's URL configuration uses regular expressions to match URLs. This allows you to create flexible and dynamic URL patterns.

Practical Implementation: Defining URL Patterns

Let's define some URL patterns in our project.

1. Open myproject/urls.py.
2. Add the following code:

Python

```python
from django.contrib import admin
from django.urls import path
from myapp import views
urlpatterns = [
    path('admin/', admin.site.urls),
    path('hello/', views.hello_view, name='hello'),
```

```
    path('products/<int:product_id>/', views.product_detail,
name='product_detail'),
]
```

In this code:

- path('admin/', admin.site.urls) maps the /admin/ URL to the admin interface.
- path('hello/', views.hello_view, name='hello') maps the /hello/ URL to the hello_view function in myapp/views.py.
- path('products/<int:product_id>/', views.product_detail, name='product_detail') maps URLs like /products/123/ to the product_detail view, passing the product ID as an integer argument.
3. Create the views that are used in the url patterns inside of the myapp/views.py file.

Python

```python
# myapp/views.py
from django.http import HttpResponse
def hello_view(request):
return HttpResponse("Hello, Django!")
def product_detail(request, product_id):
return HttpResponse(f"Product ID: {product_id}")
```

Including App URLs

For larger projects, it's best to create separate urls.py files for each app and include them in the project's main urls.py file.

1. Create a urls.py file in your app directory (myapp/urls.py).
2. Add the following code:

Python

```python
# myapp/urls.py
from django.urls import path
from . import views
urlpatterns = [
    path('', views.index, name='index'),
]
```

3. Create the view index inside of the myapp/views.py file.

Python

```python
# myapp/views.py
from django.http import HttpResponse
def index(request):
    return HttpResponse('This is the index page of my app')
```

4. Include the app's URLs in the project's urls.py file:

Python

```python
# myproject/urls.py
from django.contrib import admin
from django.urls import path, include
urlpatterns = [
    path('admin/', admin.site.urls),
```

```
    path('myapp/', include('myapp.urls')),
]
```

This setup allows you to organize your URL patterns and keep your project's urls.py file clean.

2.4 Basic Views and Template Rendering

Views and templates are essential for building dynamic web applications. Views handle the logic of your application, and templates define how that logic is presented to the user.

Understanding Views

Views are Python functions or classes that receive HTTP requests and return HTTP responses. They act as the intermediary between the model (data) and the template (presentation).

Here's a breakdown of what views do:

- **Receive HTTP Requests:** Views receive requests from users' browsers.
- **Process Data:** Views can perform various operations, such as retrieving data from the database, processing form data, or performing calculations.
- **Render Templates:** Views can render HTML templates, passing data to the template for display.
- **Return HTTP Responses:** Views return HTTP responses, which can be HTML pages, JSON data, or other types of content.

Practical Implementation: Creating a Simple View

Let's create a simple view that displays a greeting message.

1. Open myapp/views.py.
2. Add the following code:

Python

```
from django.shortcuts import render
from django.http import HttpResponse
def greeting(request):
    message = "Welcome to my Django app!"
    return render(request, 'myapp/greeting.html', {'message':
message})
```

In this code:

- We define a function called greeting that takes an request object as an argument.
- We create a message variable.
- We use the render function to render the myapp/greeting.html template, passing the message variable to the template.

Understanding Templates

Templates are HTML files that define the structure and presentation of your web pages. Django's template engine allows you to embed variables and logic within your HTML, making it easy to create dynamic content.

Here are some key features of Django templates:

- **Variables:** You can embed variables in your templates using double curly braces {{ variable }}.
- **Tags:** You can use tags to perform logic, such as loops and conditional statements. Tags are enclosed in curly braces and percent signs {% tag %}.
- **Filters:** You can use filters to modify variables, such as formatting dates or converting text to uppercase. Filters are applied using a pipe character |.

Practical Implementation: Creating a Simple Template

Let's create a template that displays the greeting message from our view.

1. Create a directory named templates inside the myapp directory.
2. Inside the templates directory, create a directory also called myapp.
3. Inside the second myapp directory, create a file named greeting.html.
4. Add the following code to greeting.html:

HTML

```
<!DOCTYPE html>
<html>
<head>
  <title>Greeting</title>
</head>
<body>
  <h1>{{ message }}</h1>
</body>
</html>
```

In this code:

- We use the {{ message }} variable to display the greeting message passed from the view.

Connecting Views and Templates

Now, let's connect our view and template by defining a URL pattern.

1. Open myproject/urls.py.
2. Add the following code:

Python

```python
from django.contrib import admin
from django.urls import path
from myapp import views
urlpatterns = [
    path('admin/', admin.site.urls),
    path('greeting/', views.greeting, name='greeting'),
]
```

3. Run the development server:

Bash

```bash
python manage.py runserver
```

4. Open your browser and navigate to http://127.0.0.1:8000/greeting/. You should see the greeting message displayed.

Real-World Example:

Imagine you're building an e-commerce website. When a user views a product page, the view retrieves the product details from the database and passes them to the template, which then displays the product information to the user.

By using views and templates, you can create dynamic web applications that respond to user requests and display data in a user-friendly way.

2.5 Introduction to Django's Command-Line Interface (manage.py)

The manage.py script is automatically created when you start a Django project. It's a command-line utility that allows you to interact with your Django project in various ways. Think of it as a control center for your Django application.

Understanding manage.py

manage.py is a Python script that uses the Django settings module to run commands in the context of your project. This means that it has access to your project's settings, database, and other resources.

Common manage.py Commands

Here are some of the most commonly used manage.py commands:

- python manage.py runserver:

- Starts the development server. This command is essential for testing your application during development.
- By default, it runs the server on http://127.0.0.1:8000/.
- You can specify a different port by running python manage.py runserver 8080.
- **python manage.py startapp <app_name>:**
  - Creates a new Django app within your project.
  - Apps are modular components that perform specific functions within your project.
  - Example: python manage.py startapp myapp.
- **python manage.py makemigrations:**
  - Creates new migrations based on changes to your models.
  - Migrations are Python files that represent changes to your database schema.
  - When you make changes to your models, you need to run this command to generate the migration files.
- **python manage.py migrate:**
  - Applies the migrations to your database, updating the schema.
  - This command actually executes the SQL commands defined in the migration files.
  - It also creates the initial tables when a project is first setup.
- **python manage.py createsuperuser:**
  - Creates a superuser account for the Django admin interface.
  - The admin interface is a powerful tool for managing your data.

- Example: python manage.py createsuperuser.
- **python manage.py shell:**
  - Opens a Python shell with access to your Django project.
  - This allows you to interact with your models, views, and other components in an interactive environment.
  - This is very useful for testing and debugging.
- **python manage.py test:**
  - Runs the unit tests for your project.
  - Testing is an essential part of software development, and Django provides tools for writing and running tests.

Practical Implementation: Using manage.py

Let's walk through some practical examples of using manage.py.

1. **Running the Development Server:**
   - Open your terminal and navigate to your project directory (the one containing manage.py).
   - Run the following command:

Bash

python manage.py runserver

- Open your browser and navigate to http://127.0.0.1:8000/. You should see the default Django welcome page.
2. **Creating a Superuser:**
   - Run the following command:

Bash

```
python manage.py createsuperuser
```

- Follow the prompts to enter a username, email, and password.
- Then navigate to http://127.0.0.1:8000/admin, and use the credentials you set to login.
3. **Using the Django Shell:**
   - Run the following command:

Bash

```
python manage.py shell
```

- You'll see a Python shell prompt.
- Now you can import your models, and interact with the database.

Python

```
from myapp.models import MyModel
MyModel.objects.all()
```

4. **Creating and Applying Migrations:**
   - If you change your models.py file, you need to create and apply migrations.
   - Run the following commands:

Bash

```
python manage.py makemigrations
python manage.py migrate
```

   - This will create and apply the necessary database changes.

Real-World Example:

Imagine you're building a large web application with multiple developers. The manage.py tool allows you to easily manage your project, run tests, and deploy changes to your database. It simplifies the development process and makes it easier to collaborate with others.

By understanding and using manage.py, you can streamline your Django development workflow and make your projects more efficient.

Chapter 3: Database Essentials with Django Models

In this chapter, we'll cover the essential aspects of working with databases in Django. We're going to understand ORMs, define models, handle migrations, use the Django admin interface, and learn how to query the database. Get ready to build your data-driven applications!

3.1 Introduction to Databases and ORMs

When you're building a web application, you'll inevitably need to store and manage data. This is where databases come in. A database is essentially an organized collection of data, designed for easy storage, retrieval, and management.[1] Think of it as a digital filing cabinet, but much more powerful.

Understanding Databases

Databases are structured in a way that allows us to perform operations like:

- **Storing Data:** Saving information for later use.[2]
- **Retrieving Data:** Querying and fetching specific data.[3]
- **Updating Data:** Modifying existing data.[4]
- **Deleting Data:** Removing unwanted data.

Common types of databases include:

- **Relational Databases (SQL):** These databases use tables with rows and columns to store data.[5] Examples include PostgreSQL, MySQL, and SQLite.[6] They use SQL (Structured Query Language) for data manipulation.

- **NoSQL Databases:** These databases use various data models other than relational tables.[7] Examples include MongoDB and Cassandra.[8] They are often used for handling large volumes of unstructured or semi-structured data.[9]

In Django, we primarily work with relational databases.

The Need for ORMs

Now, imagine you're building a web application with Django. Without an ORM, you'd have to write raw SQL queries to interact with your database. This can be tedious and error-prone.

Here's where ORMs come in. An ORM (Object-Relational Mapper) acts as a bridge between your Python code and your database.[10] It allows you to interact with the database using Python objects, abstracting away the complexities of SQL.[11]

How ORMs Work

Essentially, an ORM maps database tables to Python classes and database rows to Python objects. This means that instead of writing SQL queries, you can use Python code to perform database operations.[12]

Benefits of Using ORMs

- **Simplified Development:** ORMs make database interactions more intuitive and less verbose.[13]

- **Increased Productivity:** You can focus on your application logic rather than writing complex SQL queries.[14]
- **Improved Security:** ORMs often provide built-in protection against SQL injection attacks.
- **Database Portability:** ORMs can make it easier to switch between different database systems.[15]

Django's ORM

Django comes with its own powerful ORM, which is one of its key features.[16] It allows you to define your database models using Python classes, and Django handles the rest.[17]

Practical Implementation: Setting up a Database and a Model

Let's create a simple example to see how Django's ORM works.

1. **Ensure you have a Django project setup.** if not, follow the previous chapters instructions to setup a project.
2. **Configure your Database:**
   - In your settings.py file, configure your database settings. For example, to use SQLite:

Python

```
DATABASES = {
  'default': {
  'ENGINE': 'django.db.backends.sqlite3',
  'NAME': BASE_DIR / 'db.sqlite3',
```

```
    }
}
```

This sets up an SQLite database named db.sqlite3 in your project directory.

3. **Define a Model:**
   o In your app's models.py file, define a model:

Python


```python
# myapp/models.py
from django.db import models
class Book(models.Model):
    title = models.CharField(max_length=200)
    author = models.CharField(max_length=100)
    publication_date = models.DateField()
    def __str__(self):
    return self.title
```

This creates a Book model with fields for title, author, and publication date.

4. **Create and Apply Migrations:**
   o Run the following commands:

Bash

```bash
python manage.py makemigrations
python manage.py migrate
```

This creates and applies the necessary database tables based on your model.

5. **Interact with the Model:**
   ○ Open the Django shell:

Bash

```bash
python manage.py shell
```

Now you can interact with your model using Python code:

Python

```python
from myapp.models import Book
# Create a book
book = Book.objects.create(title="Django Basics",
author="John Doe", publication_date="2023-01-01")
# Retrieve all books
books = Book.objects.all()
print(books)
# Retrieve a specific book
book = Book.objects.get(title="Django Basics")
print(book)
```

This example shows how Django's ORM allows you to interact with the database using Python code, without writing raw SQL queries.

3.2 Defining Models and Fields

When we create a Django application, our models act as the representation of our database tables.[1] Each model we define in our models.py file corresponds to a table in the database, and the fields we define within each model correspond to the columns in that table.

Understanding Models

A Django model is a Python class that inherits from django.db.models.Model. This inheritance provides Django with the necessary tools to translate your model into database tables.

Here's a basic model structure:

Python

```
from django.db import models
class MyModel(models.Model):
    # Field definitions go here
    pass
```

Defining Fields

Fields are the attributes of your model that define the type of data that can be stored in each column of your database table.[2] Django provides a wide range of field types to handle various data types.[3]

Here are some commonly used field types:

- **CharField**: Used for short strings, such as names or titles.[4] You need to specify the `max_length` argument.
- **TextField**: Used for long strings, such as descriptions or content.[5]
- **IntegerField**: Used for integer values.[6]
- **FloatField**: Used for floating-point numbers.[7]
- **DecimalField**: Used for decimal numbers with fixed precision.[8] You need to specify `max_digits` and `decimal_places`.
- **DateField**: Used for dates.[9]
- **DateTimeField**: Used for dates and times.[10]
- **BooleanField**: Used for boolean values (True or False).[11]
- **EmailField**: Used for email addresses.[12]
- **URLField**: Used for URLs.[13]
- **ForeignKey**: Used to define a one-to-many relationship with another model.[14]
- **ManyToManyField**: Used to define a many-to-many relationship with another model.[15]
- **OneToOneField**: Used to define a one-to-one relationship with another model.[16]

Field Options

Fields can have various options that control their behavior.[17] Some common options include:

- **null=True**: Allows the field to have NULL values in the database.[18]

- blank=True: Allows the field to be blank in forms.[19]
- default: Specifies a default value for the field.[20]
- unique=True: Ensures that the field values are unique.[21]
- primary_key=True: Makes the field the primary key of the table.[22]
- choices: Provides a list of choices for the field.[23]
- max_length: Specifies the maximum length for CharField and TextField.

Practical Implementation: Creating a Model for a Blog Post

Let's create a model for a blog post with some fields and options.

Python

```python
from django.db import models
class Post(models.Model):
    title = models.CharField(max_length=200)
    content = models.TextField()
    pub_date = models.DateTimeField(auto_now_add=True)
    author = models.CharField(max_length=100)
    is_published = models.BooleanField(default=False)
    def __str__(self):
    return self.title
```

In this code:

- We define a **Post** model with fields for title, content, publication date, author, and publication status.
- auto_now_add=True automatically sets the publication date when the post is created.

- **default=False** sets the default value for the publication status to False.
- The **__str__** method returns the title of the post, which is useful for debugging and displaying objects in the admin interface.

Real-World Example:

Imagine you're building an e-commerce platform. You might create models for products, orders, and customers.

- A **Product** model could have fields for name, description, price, and stock.
- An **Order** model could have fields for customer, order date, and total amount.
- A **Customer** model could have fields for name, email, and address.

By defining models and fields, you can structure your data in a way that makes it easy to store, retrieve, and manage. This is a crucial step in building robust and scalable Django applications.

3.3 Database Migrations (Making Changes to Your Database)

When we build web applications, our data models often change over time. We might need to add new fields, modify existing ones, or even change the structure of our database tables. Django's database migrations handle these changes seamlessly.

Understanding Migrations

Migrations are essentially Python files that represent changes to your database schema. They allow Django to track and apply changes to your database in a controlled and consistent manner.

Here's why migrations are important:

- **Version Control for Databases:** Migrations act as version control for your database schema, allowing you to track changes and revert to previous versions if needed.
- **Database Independence:** Django's migrations work with various database systems, allowing you to switch databases without rewriting your database schema.
- **Collaborative Development:** Migrations facilitate collaboration among developers by ensuring that everyone's database schema is consistent.
- **Automated Schema Updates:** Migrations automate the process of updating your database schema, reducing the risk of errors.

Creating Migrations

When you make changes to your models in models.py, you need to create migrations to reflect those changes in your database.

Here's how to create migrations:

1. **Modify Your Models:**
    - Make the necessary changes to your models in models.py. For example, let's add a new field to our Post model:

Python

```python
# myapp/models.py
from django.db import models
class Post(models.Model):
    title = models.CharField(max_length=200)
    content = models.TextField()
    pub_date = models.DateTimeField(auto_now_add=True)
    author = models.CharField(max_length=100)
    is_published = models.BooleanField(default=False)
    category = models.CharField(max_length=50, null=True, blank=True) #New Field
```

2. **Create Migrations:**
    - Run the following command in your terminal:

Bash

```bash
python manage.py makemigrations
```

Django will analyze the changes to your models and create a migration file in the migrations directory of your app.

3. **Apply Migrations:**
   - Run the following command to apply the migrations to your database:

Bash

python manage.py migrate

Django will execute the SQL commands defined in the migration file to update your database schema.

Understanding Migration Files

Migration files are Python files that define the operations to be performed on your database. They typically contain functions that create, modify, or delete database tables and columns.

Here's an example of a migration file:

Python

```python
# myapp/migrations/0002_post_category.py
from django.db import migrations, models
class Migration(migrations.Migration):
    dependencies = [
    ('myapp', '0001_initial'),
    ]
    operations = [
    migrations.AddField(
```

```
    model_name='post',
    name='category',
        field=models.CharField(blank=True,  max_length=50,
null=True),
    ),
  ]
```

In this file:

- **dependencies** specifies the dependencies of this migration.
- **operations** defines the operations to be performed, such as adding a field.

Real-World Example:

Imagine you're building an e-commerce platform. Initially, you might have a **Product** model with fields for name, description, and price. Later, you might need to add a field for product images or inventory.

Using migrations, you can add these new fields without losing your existing data or disrupting your application. You can track all database changes, and revert if needed.

Handling Migration Conflicts

Sometimes, migration conflicts can occur when multiple developers make changes to the same models. Django provides tools to resolve these conflicts.

- You can manually edit the migration files to resolve conflicts.

- You can use the --merge option with makemigrations to attempt to merge conflicting migrations.

By understanding and using database migrations, you can ensure that your database schema is always up-to-date and consistent. This is crucial for building robust and scalable Django applications.

3.4 Working with the Django Admin Interface

When you build a Django application, you often need a way to manage the data stored in your database. Django's admin interface provides this functionality out of the box. It generates a web-based interface that allows you to create, read, update, and delete data from your models.

Understanding the Django Admin Interface

The Django admin interface is automatically generated based on your models. You don't need to write any HTML or CSS; Django handles the presentation for you. It's designed to be intuitive and easy to use, even for non-technical users.

Here are some key features of the admin interface:

- **Automatic Model Registration:** You register your models with the admin interface, and Django automatically creates forms and views for managing them.

- **CRUD Operations:** The admin interface provides Create, Read, Update, and Delete (CRUD) operations for your models.
- **Search and Filtering:** You can easily search and filter your data using the admin interface's built-in tools.
- **Customization:** You can customize the admin interface to fit your specific needs, such as adding custom fields, actions, and layouts.
- **User Authentication:** The admin interface includes built-in user authentication and authorization, allowing you to control who can access and modify your data.

Registering Models with the Admin Interface

To use the admin interface, you need to register your models in the admin.py file of your app.

Here's how to register a model:

1. **Open** myapp/admin.py.
2. **Add the following code:**

Python

```python
from django.contrib import admin
from .models import Post
admin.site.register(Post)
```

In this code, we're registering the Post model with the admin interface.

Accessing the Admin Interface

To access the admin interface, you need to create a superuser account.

1. **Run the following command in your terminal:**

Bash

python manage.py createsuperuser

2. **Follow the prompts to enter a username, email, and password.**
3. **Run the development server:**

Bash

python manage.py runserver

4. **Open your browser and navigate to** http://127.0.0.1:8000/admin/.
5. **Log in using the superuser credentials you created.**

You should now see the Django admin interface, which displays the models you've registered.

Customizing the Admin Interface

You can customize the admin interface to fit your specific needs. For example, you can control which fields are displayed, add search and filter options, and define custom actions.

Here's how to customize the admin interface:

1. **Create an** ModelAdmin **class in** myapp/admin.py.
2. **Use the** list_display **attribute to control which fields are displayed.**
3. **Use the** search_fields **attribute to add search functionality.**
4. **Use the** list_filter **attribute to add filter options.**

Python

```
from django.contrib import admin
from .models import Post
class PostAdmin(admin.ModelAdmin):
    list_display = ('title', 'author', 'pub_date', 'is_published')
    search_fields = ('title', 'content')
    list_filter = ('is_published', 'pub_date')
admin.site.register(Post, PostAdmin)
```

In this code:

- list_display specifies the fields to display in the list view.
- search_fields adds search functionality for the title and content fields.
- list_filter adds filter options for the publication status and publication date fields.

Real-World Example:

Imagine you're building an e-commerce platform. You might use the admin interface to manage your products, orders, and customers.

- You can create, update, and delete products using the admin interface.
- You can view and manage customer orders.
- You can manage customer accounts and addresses.

The Django admin interface provides a powerful and flexible way to manage your data, saving you time and effort.

3.5 Querying the Database with the Django ORM

When you build a web application, you'll often need to retrieve data from your database to display it to users or perform other operations. Django's ORM provides a powerful and intuitive way to query your database using Python code.

Understanding Django's ORM Querying

Django's ORM allows you to interact with your database using Python objects, abstracting away the complexities of raw SQL. This makes your code more readable, maintainable, and secure.

Here are some key concepts to understand:

- **QuerySets:** QuerySets are the bread and butter of Django's ORM. They represent a collection of objects from your database. When you perform a query, you get back a QuerySet. QuerySets are lazy, which means they are not evaluated until you actually need the data.

- **Managers:** Managers provide the interface for database query operations to your models. The default manager is objects, which you use to access the database.
- **Filters:** Filters allow you to narrow down your queries based on specific criteria.
- **Lookups:** Lookups are used within filters to specify the type of comparison you want to perform.

Retrieving Objects

Let's start with retrieving objects from your database.

1. **Retrieving All Objects:**
   - To retrieve all objects from a model, you can use the all() method.

Python

```
from myapp.models import Post
posts = Post.objects.all()
for post in posts:
print(post.title)
```

2. **Retrieving a Single Object:**
   - To retrieve a single object, you can use the get() method.
   - The get() method raises an exception if no object matches the query or if multiple objects match.
   - To prevent exceptions when an object might not exist use get_object_or_404()

Python

```
from myapp.models import Post
from django.shortcuts import get_object_or_404
post = get_object_or_404(Post, pk=1) #using the primary key.
print(post.title)
```

Filtering Objects

Filters allow you to narrow down your queries based on specific criteria.

1. **Filtering by Field Values:**
   - You can use the filter() method to filter objects based on field values.

Python

```
from myapp.models import Post
published_posts = Post.objects.filter(is_published=True)
for post in published_posts:
 print(post.title)
```

2. **Using Lookups:**
   - Lookups allow you to specify the type of comparison you want to perform.
   - Common lookups include **exact, iexact, contains, icontains, gt, gte, lt, lte, in, and** range.

Python

```
from myapp.models import Post
recent_posts                                                    =
Post.objects.filter(pub_date__gte='2023-01-01')         #posts
published on or after 2023-01-01
for post in recent_posts:
print(post.title)
```

   3. **Chaining Filters:**
     ○ You can chain multiple filters to create complex queries.

Python

```
from myapp.models import Post
filtered_posts                                                  =
Post.objects.filter(is_published=True).filter(author='John
Doe')
for post in filtered_posts:
  print(post.title)
```

Ordering Objects

You can use the order_by() method to order objects based on field values.

Python

```
from myapp.models import Post
```

```python
ordered_posts = Post.objects.order_by('pub_date') #orders
by publication date, oldest to newest.
ordered_posts_desc = Post.objects.order_by('-pub_date')
#orders by publication date, newest to oldest.
for post in ordered_posts:
    print(post.title)
```

Creating, Updating, and Deleting Objects

1. **Creating Objects:**
   - You can create new objects using the create()
     method.

Python

```python
from myapp.models import Post
new_post = Post.objects.create(title='New Post',
content='This is a new post.', author='Jane Smith',
is_published=True)
```

2. **Updating Objects:**
   - You can update existing objects by modifying
     their attributes and calling the save() method.

Python

```python
from myapp.models import Post
post = Post.objects.get(pk=1)
post.title = 'Updated Post'
```

```
post.save()
```

3. **Deleting Objects:**
   - You can delete objects using the delete() method.

Python

```
from myapp.models import Post
post = Post.objects.get(pk=1)
post.delete()
```

Real-World Example:

Imagine you're building an e-commerce platform. You might use Django's ORM to:

- Retrieve all products in a specific category.
- Filter products based on price range.
- Order products by popularity or rating.
- Update product inventory.

By understanding how to query your database using Django's ORM, you can build powerful and efficient web applications.

Chapter 4: Advanced Model Techniques

In this chapter, we're going to explore how to create complex data structures using model relationships, inheritance, custom methods, and more. We'll also learn how to optimize our database queries for better performance. Get ready to build more sophisticated Django applications!

4.1 Model Relationships (One-to-One, One-to-Many, Many-to-Many)

In Django, we often need to define how different models relate to each other.[1] These relationships are the backbone of your application's data structure, allowing you to create complex and interconnected data models.[2] Django provides three types of relationships: One-to-One, One-to-Many, and Many-to-Many.[3]

One-to-One Relationships (OneToOneField)

A One-to-One relationship is used when each instance of one model is related to exactly one instance of another model. Think of it as a unique pairing.

- **Use Case:** User profiles, where each user has one profile, and each profile belongs to one user.[4]
- **Implementation:** We use the OneToOneField to define this relationship.

Python

```python
from django.db import models
from django.contrib.auth.models import User
class Profile(models.Model):
    user    =    models.OneToOneField(User,
on_delete=models.CASCADE)
    bio = models.TextField(blank=True)
    birth_date = models.DateField(null=True, blank=True)
    def __str__(self):
    return self.user.username
```

In this example:

- user   =   models.OneToOneField(User, on_delete=models.CASCADE) establishes a One-to-One relationship between the Profile and User models.
- on_delete=models.CASCADE specifies that if a user is deleted, their profile should also be deleted.

One-to-Many Relationships (ForeignKey)

A One-to-Many relationship (also known as a ForeignKey relationship) is used when each instance of one model is related to multiple instances of another model. Think of a blog author who has many blog posts.

- **Use Case:** Blog posts and authors, where each author can have multiple posts, but each post has only one author.
- **Implementation:** We use the ForeignKey to define this relationship.

Python

```python
from django.db import models
from django.contrib.auth.models import User
class Post(models.Model):
    title = models.CharField(max_length=200)
    content = models.TextField()
    author = models.ForeignKey(User, on_delete=models.CASCADE)
    pub_date = models.DateTimeField(auto_now_add=True)
    def __str__(self):
    return self.title
```

In this example:

- author = models.ForeignKey(User, on_delete=models.CASCADE) establishes a One-to-Many relationship between the Post and User models.
- Each Post instance has a author field that points to a User instance.

Many-to-Many Relationships (ManyToManyField)

A Many-to-Many relationship is used when each instance of one model is related to multiple instances of another model, and vice versa. Think of blog posts and tags, where each post can have multiple tags, and each tag can be applied to multiple posts.

- **Use Case:** Blog posts and tags, products and categories.
- **Implementation:** We use the ManyToManyField to define this relationship.

Python

```python
from django.db import models
class Tag(models.Model):
    name = models.CharField(max_length=50)
    def __str__(self):
    return self.name
class Post(models.Model):
    title = models.CharField(max_length=200)
    content = models.TextField()
    tags = models.ManyToManyField(Tag)
    pub_date = models.DateTimeField(auto_now_add=True)
    def __str__(self):
        return self.title
```

In this example:

- tags = models.ManyToManyField(Tag) establishes a Many-to-Many relationship between the Post and Tag models.
- Each Post instance can have multiple Tag instances, and each Tag instance can be associated with multiple Post instances.

Practical Implementation: Creating and Querying Relationships

Let's see how to create and query these relationships.

1. **Create Objects:**

Python

```python
from django.contrib.auth.models import User
from myapp.models import Profile, Post, Tag
```

```python
# Create a User and Profile
user        =        User.objects.create_user(username='john',
password='password')
profile = Profile.objects.create(user=user, bio='John\'s bio')
# Create a Post
post     =     Post.objects.create(title='My     First     Post',
content='Hello, Django!', author=user)
#Create some tags.
tag1 = Tag.objects.create(name='Django')
tag2 = Tag.objects.create(name='Python')
#Add the tags to the post.
post.tags.add(tag1, tag2)
```

2. **Query Relationships:**

Python

```python
# Get the user's profile
john_profile = user.profile
print(john_profile.bio)
# Get the post's author
post_author = post.author
print(post_author.username)
# Get the post's tags
post_tags = post.tags.all()
for tag in post_tags:
    print(tag.name)
# Get all posts with the Django tag.
django_posts = Post.objects.filter(tags__name='Django')
for p in django_posts:
    print(p.title)
```

By understanding and using these model relationships, you can create complex and interconnected data structures in your Django applications.

4.2 Model Inheritance

Model inheritance in Django is a way to create new models that inherit fields and methods from existing models. This allows you to avoid code duplication and create more organized and maintainable applications. Django provides two main types of model inheritance: abstract base classes and multi-table inheritance.

Abstract Base Classes

Abstract base classes are used to define common fields and methods that are shared among multiple models. These classes are not used to create database tables themselves. Instead, they serve as a blueprint for other models.

- **Use Case:** You have multiple models that share common fields, such as created_at and updated_at.
- **Implementation:** You create an abstract base class by setting abstract = True in the Meta class.

Python

```python
from django.db import models
class TimeStampedModel(models.Model):
    created_at = models.DateTimeField(auto_now_add=True)
    updated_at = models.DateTimeField(auto_now=True)
```

```
    class Meta:
    abstract = True
class Article(TimeStampedModel):
  title = models.CharField(max_length=200)
  content = models.TextField()
  def __str__(self):
  return self.title
class Comment(TimeStampedModel):
  text = models.TextField()
              article    =    models.ForeignKey(Article,
on_delete=models.CASCADE)
  def __str__(self):
  return self.text
```

In this example:

- **TimeStampedModel** is an abstract base class that defines created_at and updated_at fields.
- **Article** and **Comment** models inherit from **TimeStampedModel** and automatically get these fields.
- No database table is created for TimeStampedModel.

Multi-Table Inheritance

Multi-table inheritance creates a separate database table for each model in the inheritance hierarchy. This allows you to create specialized models that inherit from a more general model.

- **Use Case:** You have a general model, such as Place, and you want to create more specific models, such as Restaurant and Hotel.

- **Implementation:** You create a model that inherits from another model.

Python

```python
from django.db import models
class Place(models.Model):
    name = models.CharField(max_length=50)
    address = models.CharField(max_length=80)
    def __str__(self):
    return self.name
class Restaurant(Place):
    serves_hot_dogs = models.BooleanField(default=False)
    serves_pizza = models.BooleanField(default=False)
    def __str__(self):
     return f"{self.name} Restaurant"
class Hotel(Place):
    rooms = models.IntegerField()
    stars = models.IntegerField()
    def __str__(self):
    return f"{self.name} Hotel"
```

In this example:

- Place is a general model.
- Restaurant and Hotel models inherit from Place.
- Django creates separate database tables for Place, Restaurant, and Hotel.
- The Restaurant and Hotel tables include all the fields from Place, as well as their own specific fields.

Practical Implementation: Creating and Querying Inherited Models

Let's see how to create and query these inherited models.

1. **Create Objects:**

Python

```
from myapp.models import Article, Comment, Restaurant, Hotel
# Create an Article and Comment
article = Article.objects.create(title='Django Inheritance', content='Exploring model inheritance.')
comment = Comment.objects.create(text='Great article!', article=article)
# Create a Restaurant and Hotel
restaurant = Restaurant.objects.create(name='Pizza Place', address='123 Main St', serves_pizza=True)
hotel = Hotel.objects.create(name='Luxury Hotel', address='456 Oak Ave', rooms=100, stars=5)
```

2. **Query Objects:**

Python

```
# Get all Articles and Comments
articles = Article.objects.all()
comments = Comment.objects.all()
for art in articles:
    print (art.title, art.created_at)
for comm in comments:
    print(comm.text, comm.article)
```

```
# Get all Restaurants and Hotels
restaurants = Restaurant.objects.all()
hotels = Hotel.objects.all()

for rest in restaurants:
    print(rest.name, rest.serves_pizza)
for hot in hotels:
    print(hot.name, hot.rooms)
# Get all Places
places = Place.objects.all()
for place in places:
    print(place.name)
# Get all hotels that have more than 50 rooms.
big_hotels = Hotel.objects.filter(rooms__gt = 50)
for big_hotel in big_hotels:
    print(big_hotel.name)
```

By understanding and using model inheritance, you can create more organized and maintainable Django applications.

4.3 Custom Model Methods and Properties

When building Django applications, you'll often encounter scenarios where you need to add custom logic or compute values based on your model's data. Custom model methods and properties provide a way to do this directly within your model definitions.

Understanding Model Methods

Model methods are functions that are defined within a model class. They can be used to perform operations on model instances, such as formatting data, performing calculations, or interacting with other models.

Here's how to define a model method:

Python

```python
from django.db import models

class Product(models.Model):
    name = models.CharField(max_length=200)
    price = models.DecimalField(max_digits=10,
decimal_places=2)
    discount = models.DecimalField(max_digits=5,
decimal_places=2, default=0)
    def discounted_price(self):
    """Calculates the discounted price of the product."""
    return self.price * (1 - self.discount)
    def __str__(self):
    return self.name
```

In this example:

- We define a Product model with name, price, and discount fields.
- We define a discounted_price method that calculates the discounted price of the product.
- The self parameter refers to the current instance of the Product model.

Understanding Model Properties

Model properties are attributes that are computed dynamically. They provide read-only access to computed values, making your model's data more accessible and organized.

Here's how to define a model property:

Python

```python
from django.db import models
class Order(models.Model):
  quantity = models.IntegerField()
      unit_price = models.DecimalField(max_digits=10, decimal_places=2)
  @property
  def total_price(self):
  """Calculates the total price of the order."""
  return self.quantity * self.unit_price
  def __str__(self):
  return f"Order {self.id}"
```

In this example:

- We define an Order model with quantity and unit_price fields.
- We define a total_price property using the @property decorator.
- The total_price property calculates the total price of the order dynamically.

Practical Implementation: Using Model Methods and Properties

Let's see how to use model methods and properties in practice.

1. **Create Objects:**

Python

```python
from myapp.models import Product, Order
# Create a Product
product = Product.objects.create(name='Laptop', price=1000, discount=0.1)
# Create an Order
order = Order.objects.create(quantity=2, unit_price=50)
```

2. **Use Model Methods:**

Python

```python
# Calculate the discounted price
discounted_price = product.discounted_price()
print(f"Discounted price: ${discounted_price}")
```

3. **Use Model Properties:**

Python

```python
# Access the total price
total_price = order.total_price
print(f"Total price: ${total_price}")
```

Real-World Example:

Imagine you're building an e-commerce platform. You might use model methods and properties to:

- Calculate the total price of an order, including discounts and taxes.
- Format dates and times for display.
- Generate product URLs.
- Check if a product is in stock.

For example, you could add a method to a model to check if the item is in stock.

Python

```python
from django.db import models
class InventoryItem(models.Model):
    name = models.CharField(max_length=200)
    quantity = models.IntegerField()
    def is_in_stock(self):
        return self.quantity > 0
```

By using custom model methods and properties, you can encapsulate business logic and computed values within your models, making your code more organized, maintainable, and reusable. This practice results in cleaner and more efficient Django applications.

4.4 Using Managers and QuerySets Effectively

When working with Django models, Managers and QuerySets are essential tools for retrieving and manipulating data. Managers provide the interface for database query operations, while QuerySets represent collections of objects from your database.

Understanding Managers

Managers are classes that provide the interface for database query operations to your models. Every Django model has at least one manager, called objects, which is automatically created by Django.

Here's how to create a custom manager:

Python

```python
from django.db import models

class PublishedPostManager(models.Manager):

    def get_queryset(self):

    return super().get_queryset().filter(is_published=True)

class Post(models.Model):

    title = models.CharField(max_length=200)

    content = models.TextField()

    is_published = models.BooleanField(default=False)
```

```python
objects = models.Manager() # The default manager.

published = PublishedPostManager() # Our custom manager.

def __str__(self):

return self.title
```

In this example:

- We create a custom manager called **PublishedPostManager** that overrides the get_queryset() method to return only published posts.
- We add this manager to our Post model as published.

Understanding QuerySets

QuerySets represent collections of objects from your database. They are lazy, which means they are not evaluated until you actually need the data.

Here are some common QuerySet methods:

- all(): Returns all objects from the database.
- filter(): Returns objects that match the given lookup parameters.
- exclude(): Returns objects that do not match the given lookup parameters.
- order_by(): Orders the objects by the given field(s).
- values(): Returns a QuerySet that returns dictionaries instead of model instances.
- values_list(): Returns a QuerySet that returns tuples instead of model instances.

- annotate(): Adds annotations to the QuerySet, allowing you to perform aggregations.
- aggregate(): Returns a dictionary containing aggregations over the QuerySet.
- get(): Returns a single object that matches the given lookup parameters.
- first(): Returns the first object in the QuerySet.
- last(): Returns the last object in the QuerySet.
- count(): Returns the number of objects in the QuerySet.
- exists(): Returns True if the QuerySet contains any objects.

Practical Implementation: Using Managers and QuerySets

Let's see how to use managers and QuerySets in practice.

1. **Create Objects:**

Python

```python
from myapp.models import Post

# Create some posts

Post.objects.create(title='Post 1', content='Content 1', is_published=True)

Post.objects.create(title='Post 2', content='Content 2', is_published=False)

Post.objects.create(title='Post 3', content='Content 3', is_published=True)
```

2. Use Custom Managers:

Python

```python
from myapp.models import Post
# Get all published posts using the custom manager
published_posts = Post.published.all()
for post in published_posts:
print(post.title)
```

3. Use QuerySet Methods:

Python

```python
from myapp.models import Post
from django.db.models import Count
# Filter posts by title
filtered_posts = Post.objects.filter(title__icontains='Post')
for post in filtered_posts:
print(post.title)
# Order posts by title
ordered_posts = Post.objects.order_by('title')
for post in ordered_posts:
```

```python
print(post.title)

# Aggregate posts by published status

published_count                                         =
Post.objects.filter(is_published=True).count()

print(f"Published posts: {published_count}")


# Annotate posts with word count

annotated_posts                                         =
Post.objects.annotate(word_count=Count('content'))

for post in annotated_posts:

print(f"{post.title}: {post.word_count} words")
```

Example:

Imagine you're building a blog application. You might use custom managers to:

- Retrieve only published posts.
- Retrieve posts from a specific author.
- Retrieve posts with a specific tag.

You might use QuerySet methods to:

- Filter posts by title or content.
- Order posts by publication date or title.
- Aggregate posts by author or category.

- Annotate posts with word count or comment count.

By mastering the use of Managers and QuerySets, you can optimize your database queries and build more efficient and maintainable Django applications.

4.5 Advanced Database Queries and Aggregations

Django's ORM is quite powerful and provides tools for performing complex database operations beyond simple retrieval. We'll focus on two key areas: aggregations and complex lookups.

Aggregations

Aggregations allow you to compute summary statistics over a set of objects. For example, you might want to calculate the average price of all products, the highest salary among employees, or the total number of orders placed.

Django's aggregate() function is used to perform aggregations. It returns a dictionary containing the computed values.

Here are some commonly used aggregation functions:

- Avg: Calculates the average value.
- Count: Counts the number of objects.
- Max: Finds the maximum value.
- Min: Finds the minimum value.

- **Sum**: Calculates the sum of values.

Practical Implementation: Performing Aggregations

Let's see how to use aggregations in practice.

1. **Define Models:**

Python

```python
from django.db import models
from django.db.models import Avg, Count, Max, Min, Sum
class Product(models.Model):
    name = models.CharField(max_length=200)
    price = models.DecimalField(max_digits=10,
decimal_places=2)
    stock = models.IntegerField()
    def __str__(self):
    return self.name
class Order(models.Model):
    product = models.ForeignKey(Product,
on_delete=models.CASCADE)
    quantity = models.IntegerField()
    def __str__(self):
    return f"Order for {self.quantity} of {self.product.name}"
```

2. **Create Objects:**

Python

```python
# Create some products
product1 = Product.objects.create(name='Laptop',
price=1200, stock=10)
```

```python
product2 = Product.objects.create(name='Mouse', price=25,
stock=100)
product3    =    Product.objects.create(name='Keyboard',
price=50, stock=50)
# Create some orders
Order.objects.create(product=product1, quantity=2)
Order.objects.create(product=product1, quantity=1)
Order.objects.create(product=product2, quantity=5)
Order.objects.create(product=product3, quantity=3)
```

3. **Perform Aggregations:**

Python

```python
from myapp.models import Product, Order
from django.db.models import Avg, Count, Max, Min, Sum
# Calculate the average price of all products
average_price = Product.objects.aggregate(Avg('price'))
print(f"Average price: ${average_price['price__avg']}")
# Calculate the total number of products
total_products = Product.objects.aggregate(Count('id'))
print(f"Total products: {total_products['id__count']}")
# Find the most expensive product
max_price = Product.objects.aggregate(Max('price'))
print(f"Max price: ${max_price['price__max']}")
# Calculate the total quantity of products ordered
total_quantity = Order.objects.aggregate(Sum('quantity'))
print(f"Total          quantity          ordered:
{total_quantity['quantity__sum']}")
# Calculate the average quantity of products ordered for
each product
```

```python
average_quantities                                                =
Order.objects.values('product__name').annotate(Avg('quanti
ty'))
for item in average_quantities:
    print(f"Average quantity for {item['product__name']}:
{item['quantity__avg']}")
```

Complex Lookups

Complex lookups allow you to perform more sophisticated filtering of your data. You can combine multiple lookups using logical operators (AND, OR, NOT) and use lookups across related models.

Django provides the following tools for complex lookups:

- **Q objects:** Q objects allow you to build complex queries using logical operators.
- **F objects:** F objects allow you to refer to model fields in queries.

Practical Implementation: Using Complex Lookups

Let's see how to use complex lookups in practice.

1. **Using Q objects:**

Python

```python
from django.db.models import Q
from myapp.models import Product
# Find products that are either expensive or low in stock
expensive_or_low_stock = Product.objects.filter(
Q(price__gt=1000) | Q(stock__lt=20)
```

```
)
for product in expensive_or_low_stock:
print(f"{product.name}: Price - ${product.price}, Stock -
{product.stock}")
# Find products that are expensive and not low in stock
expensive_and_not_low_stock = Product.objects.filter(
Q(price__gt=1000) & ~Q(stock__lt=20)
)
for product in expensive_and_not_low_stock:
    print(f"{product.name}: Price - ${product.price}, Stock -
{product.stock}")
```

2. Using F objects:

Python

```
from django.db.models import F
from myapp.models import Product
# Find products where the price is greater than the average
price
average_price                                    =
Product.objects.aggregate(Avg('price'))['price__avg']
expensive_products                               =
Product.objects.filter(price__gt=F('price')) #This will filter
nothing.
expensive_products_2                             =
Product.objects.filter(price__gt=average_price)  #This will
return the products with price greater than the average.
for product in expensive_products_2:
print(f"{product.name}: Price - ${product.price}")
# Increase the stock of all products by 10
Product.objects.update(stock=F('stock') + 10)
```

```
for product in Product.objects.all():
    print(f"{product.name}: Stock - {product.stock}")
```

Real-World Example:

Imagine you're building an e-commerce platform. You might use:

- Aggregations to calculate sales statistics, such as average order value, total revenue, or the number of orders placed in a given period.
- Complex lookups to filter products based on multiple criteria, such as price range, availability, and category, or to find customers who have placed orders above a certain value and live in a specific region.

By mastering advanced database queries and aggregations, you can extract valuable insights from your data and build more sophisticated and data-driven Django applications.

Chapter 5: Views and URL Routing

Let's talk about how to handle user requests and display information in Django! In this chapter, we'll learn about views, which are the logic handlers of your application, and URLs, which define how users access those views. We'll cover function-based and class-based views, URL patterns, HTTP request handling, form processing, and sessions. Get ready to build interactive and dynamic web pages!

5.1 Function-Based Views vs. Class-Based Views

In Django, a view is the part of your application that handles the logic for processing a user's request and returning a response.[2] This response is most commonly an HTML page, but it can also be JSON data, a redirect, or something else.[3]

Function-Based Views (FBVs)

Function-based views are, as the name suggests, Python functions.[4] They take an HttpRequest object as their first argument and return an HttpResponse object. They are straightforward and often easier to grasp, especially for simple tasks.

Here's a basic example:

Python

```
from django.http import HttpResponse
from django.shortcuts import render
```

```
def my_view(request):
    # Logic to process the request
    data = {'message': 'Hello from a function-based view!'}
    return render(request, 'my_template.html', data)
```

In this code:

- We define a function called my_view that takes request as an argument.
- We create a dictionary data to pass to the template.
- We use render to combine the template my_template.html with the data and return an HttpResponse.

Function-based views are great for:

- Simple logic that doesn't need much reuse.
- Quickly prototyping or building small applications.
- Situations where you prefer the explicit control of a function.

Class-Based Views (CBVs)

Class-based views, on the other hand, are Python classes that inherit from Django's built-in view classes.[5] They provide a more structured way to handle common view patterns, especially when dealing with different HTTP methods (GET, POST, etc.).

Here's an equivalent example to the function-based view above, but using a class-based view:

Python

```python
from django.views.generic import TemplateView
class MyView(TemplateView):
    template_name = 'my_template.html'
    def get_context_data(self, **kwargs):
    context = super().get_context_data(**kwargs)
    context['message'] = 'Hello from a class-based view!'
    return context
```

In this code:

- We define a class MyView that inherits from TemplateView.
- We set the template_name attribute to specify the template to use.
- We override the get_context_data method to add data to the template context.

Class-based views are beneficial for:

- Handling different HTTP methods (e.g., displaying a form with GET and processing it with POST).
- Reusing view logic across multiple parts of your application.
- Implementing common patterns like displaying lists of objects, creating forms, or displaying detail pages.

Django provides several built-in class-based views, such as:

- TemplateView: For simply rendering a template.
- ListView: For displaying a list of objects.
- DetailView: For displaying details of a single object.
- CreateView, UpdateView, DeleteView: For handling forms to create, update, and delete objects.

Key Differences and When to Choose

- **Explicit vs. Implicit:** Function-based views are explicit; you write out the logic step by step.[6] Class-based views are more implicit, relying on inheritance and method overriding.[7]
- **Reusability:** Class-based views promote reusability through inheritance.[8] You can easily extend built-in views or create your own base views.
- **Organization:** Class-based views can help organize complex view logic, especially when handling multiple HTTP methods.[9]
- **Complexity:** For very simple views, function-based views can be more concise. As views become more complex, class-based views often lead to cleaner code.

Practical Example: Handling GET and POST

Let's illustrate the difference with a common scenario: handling a form submission.

Function-Based View:

Python

```python
from django.shortcuts import render
from django.http import HttpResponseRedirect

def my_form_view(request):
    if request.method == 'POST':
        # Process the form data
        form_data = request.POST
        # ... your logic here ...
```

```
    return HttpResponseRedirect('/success/')  # Redirect on
success
  else:
    # Display the form
    return render(request, 'my_form.html')
```

Class-Based View:

Python

```
from django.views.generic import FormView
from django.http import HttpResponseRedirect
from django import forms
class MyForm(forms.Form):
  my_field = forms.CharField(label="Enter something")
class MyFormView(FormView):
  template_name = 'my_form.html'
  form_class = MyForm
  success_url = '/success/'
  def form_valid(self, form):
  # Process the form data
    form_data = form.cleaned_data
    # ... your logic here ...
    return super().form_valid(form)
```

In the class-based view example:

- We use the FormView which handles both GET and POST requests.
- The form_valid method is automatically called when the form is submitted and valid.

This demonstrates how class-based views can streamline common patterns.

Ultimately, the choice between function-based and class-based views depends on the specific requirements of your view. For simple tasks, function-based views are often sufficient. For more complex and reusable logic, class-based views provide a powerful and organized approach.

5.2 URL Patterns and Regular Expressions

When a user types a URL in their browser (like http://www.example.com/blog/my-post/), Django needs to figure out which view function or class should be responsible for generating the response. This is the job of the URL configuration.

URL Patterns

In its simplest form, a URL pattern is a direct mapping between a URL path and a view. You define these patterns in your urls.py file. Django checks the requested URL against these patterns, and when it finds a match, it executes the associated view.

Here's a basic example:

Python

```
from django.urls import path
from . import views
urlpatterns = [
```

```
    path('about/', views.about_page, name='about'),
    path('contact/', views.contact_page, name='contact'),
]
```

In this code:

- We use path() to define URL patterns.
- The first argument to path() is the URL path ('about/', 'contact/').
- The second argument is the view function that should handle requests to that path (views.about_page, views.contact_page).
- The name argument provides a convenient way to refer to this URL pattern in your code (more on this later).

If a user visits http://www.example.com/about/, Django will execute the about_page view.

Capturing Values in URLs

Often, you'll want to capture parts of the URL and pass them to your view. For example, in a blog, you might want URLs like /blog/2023/12/my-post/, where 2023 and 12 represent the year and month of the post.

Django allows you to capture these values using angle brackets:

Python

```
from django.urls import path
from . import views
urlpatterns = [
```

```python
    path('blog/<int:year>/<int:month>/<slug:post>/',
views.blog_post, name='blog_post'),
]
```

Here's what's happening:

- <int:year>: This captures an integer value from the URL and passes it to the year argument of the blog_post view.
- <int:month>: Similarly, this captures an integer for the month.
- <slug:post>: This captures a "slug" (a URL-friendly string) for the post title and passes it to the post argument.

The int and slug parts are called "path converters." Django provides several built-in converters, and you can even define your own.

Using Regular Expressions

For more complex URL matching, you can use regular expressions. Regular expressions are a powerful way to define patterns in strings. Django's re_path() function allows you to use regular expressions in your URL configuration.

Here's an example:

Python

```python
from django.urls import path, re_path
from . import views
urlpatterns = [
```

```python
        re_path(r'^articles/(?P<year>[0-9]{4})/$',
views.article_year, name='article_year'),

re_path(r'^articles/(?P<year>[0-9]{4})/(?P<month>[0-9]{2})/
$', views.article_month, name='article_month'),
]
```

Let's break down the regular expressions:

- r'^articles/': This matches any URL that starts with /articles/. The r prefix indicates a "raw string," which is recommended for regular expressions in Python.
- (?P<year>[0-9]{4}): This is a named capturing group.
  - ?P<year>: This names the captured group "year."
  - [0-9]{4}: This matches exactly four digits (0-9).
- /$': This matches the end of the URL. The $ symbol signifies the end.
- (?P<month>[0-9]{2}): This captures a two-digit month.

In this example, URLs like /articles/2023/ and /articles/2023/12/ would match. The captured year and month values would be passed as arguments to the corresponding views (article_year and article_month).

Why name is Important

The name argument in path() and re_path() is extremely useful. It allows you to refer to your URL patterns in your Django code (especially in templates) without hardcoding the URLs themselves. This makes your code more flexible and maintainable.

For example, if you change the URL pattern for your about page, you only need to update it in urls.py. Any code that uses the name='about' will automatically use the new URL.

You can use the reverse() function to get the URL for a named pattern:

Python

```python
from django.urls import reverse
about_url = reverse('about')  # This will return '/about/'
```

And in templates:

HTML

```html
<a href="{% url 'about' %}">About Us</a>
```

Practical Example: A Simple Blog URL Configuration

Here's a more complete example of a urls.py file for a simple blog:

Python

```python
from django.urls import path, re_path
from . import views
urlpatterns = [
    path('', views.home, name='home'),  # Home page
    path('about/', views.about, name='about'),
                path('post/<slug:slug>/',    views.post_detail,
name='post_detail'),  # Post detail
```

```
        re_path(r'^archive/(?P<year>[0-9]{4})/$',
views.post_archive_year,    name='post_archive_year'),    #
Archive by year

re_path(r'^archive/(?P<year>[0-9]{4})/(?P<month>[0-9]{2})/
$', views.post_archive_month, name='post_archive_month'),
# Archive by year and month
]
```

This configuration handles:

- The home page (/)
- The about page (/about/)
- Individual post pages (/post/my-first-post/)
- Yearly archives (/archive/2023/)
- Monthly archives (/archive/2023/12/)

Django's URL configuration is a powerful tool for mapping URLs to your application's logic. By understanding URL patterns, path converters, and regular expressions, you can create flexible and user-friendly web applications.

5.3 Handling HTTP Requests (GET, POST, PUT, DELETE)

HTTP (Hypertext Transfer Protocol) is the foundation of data communication for the World Wide Web. When a user interacts with a website – whether by clicking a link, submitting a form, or simply loading a page – HTTP requests and responses are exchanged between the user's browser and the web server.

Different HTTP methods are used to perform different types of actions.[1] Understanding these methods is crucial for building robust and well-behaved web applications. The most common methods are:

- **GET:**
    - The GET method is used to *retrieve* data from a server.[2]
    - When you type a URL in your browser's address bar and press Enter, the browser sends a GET request to the server.
    - GET requests are generally considered safe, meaning they should not have side effects on the server (like modifying data).[3]
    - Data is typically sent to the server as part of the URL itself (query parameters).[4]
- **POST:**
    - The POST method is used to *submit* data to a server to create or update a resource.[5]
    - When you submit a form on a web page, the browser often sends a POST request to the server.[6]
    - POST requests can have side effects on the server (like creating a new entry in a database).[7]
    - Data is sent to the server in the body of the HTTP request.[8]
- **PUT:**
    - The PUT method is used to *update* an existing resource on the server.[9]

- It's similar to POST, but the key difference is that PUT is intended for updating a resource at a specific URL.
  - If the resource doesn't exist at that URL, a PUT request *might* create it, but this behavior is not guaranteed.
- **DELETE:**
  - The DELETE method is used to *delete* a resource on the server.[10]
  - As the name suggests, it's used when you want to remove something, like a blog post or a user account.

Handling HTTP Methods in Django Views

Django views are responsible for handling HTTP requests.[11] You can write your view logic to respond differently based on the HTTP method used in the request.

1. Function-Based Views

In function-based views, you typically use conditional statements to check the request method and execute the appropriate logic.

Python

```
from        django.http        import        HttpResponse,
HttpResponseRedirect
from django.shortcuts import render
from .forms import MyForm  # Assume you have a form
defined
```

```
def my_view(request):
    if request.method == 'GET':
        # Process a GET request (e.g., display a form)
        form = MyForm()
        return render(request, 'my_template.html', {'form':
form})
    elif request.method == 'POST':
        # Process a POST request (e.g., handle form submission)
        form = MyForm(request.POST)
        if form.is_valid():
            # Form data is valid, do something with it
            # ... your logic here ...
            return HttpResponseRedirect('/success/') # Redirect
on success
        else:
            # Form data is invalid, display errors
            return render(request, 'my_template.html', {'form':
form})
    else:
        # Handle other HTTP methods (PUT, DELETE, etc.)
        return HttpResponse(status=405)  # Method Not
Allowed
```

In this code:

- We check **request.method** to determine the HTTP method.
- For GET requests, we display a form.
- For POST requests, we process the form data.[12]
- We return an **HttpResponse** or **HttpResponseRedirect** as appropriate.

- status=405 indicates that the server understands the request method but the target resource does not support this method.

2. Class-Based Views

Class-based views provide a more structured way to handle different HTTP methods.[13] Django's built-in class-based views (like View, FormView, etc.) have methods like get(), post(), put(), and delete() that you can override to handle specific HTTP methods.

Python

```python
from django.views import View
from django.http import HttpResponse, HttpResponseRedirect
from django.shortcuts import render
from .forms import MyForm

class MyView(View):
    def get(self, request):
        # Process a GET request
        form = MyForm()
        return render(request, 'my_template.html', {'form': form})
    def post(self, request):
        # Process a POST request
        form = MyForm(request.POST)
        if form.is_valid():
        # Form data is valid, do something with it
            # ... your logic here ...
```

```
    return HttpResponseRedirect('/success/')
else:
    # Form data is invalid, display errors
        return render(request, 'my_template.html', {'form':
form})
  def put(self, request):
    # Process a PUT request
        return HttpResponse(status=405)  # Method Not
Allowed (example)
  def delete(self, request):
    # Process a DELETE request
        return HttpResponse(status=405)  # Method Not
Allowed (example)
```

In this code:

- We inherit from Django's base View class.
- We define separate methods for get(), post(), put(), and delete().
- Django automatically calls the appropriate method based on the request's HTTP method.

Practical Examples

- **GET:**
    - Displaying a web page.
    - Fetching data from an API.
    - Displaying search results.
- **POST:**
    - Submitting a registration form.
    - Creating a new blog post.
    - Adding an item to a shopping cart.
- **PUT:**

- o Updating a user's profile information.
- o Modifying a product's details in an inventory system.
- **DELETE:**
  - o Removing a blog post.
  - o Deleting a user account.
  - o Deleting an item from a shopping cart.

Important Considerations

- **Idempotency:** GET, PUT, and DELETE requests are generally expected to be idempotent.[14] This means that performing the same request multiple times should have the same outcome as performing it once. POST requests, on the other hand, are not required to be idempotent.
- **Security:** Be mindful of security implications when handling different HTTP methods. For example, ensure that only authorized users can perform PUT or DELETE requests.
- **RESTful APIs:** When building RESTful APIs, it's crucial to adhere to the conventions of HTTP methods to ensure consistency and predictability.

By understanding how to handle HTTP requests in Django, you can build web applications that interact effectively with users and other systems.

5.4 Form Handling and Validation

When you build a web application, you'll often need to collect information from users. Whether it's a simple contact form, a user registration form, or a complex data entry interface, forms are the tool you'll use. Django's form handling capabilities make this process much easier and safer.

Understanding Django Forms

Django forms are more than just HTML. They are Python classes that define the fields of your form, their data types, how they should be rendered, and the rules for validating the user's input. This separation of concerns is a key strength of Django's approach.

Here's a breakdown of what Django forms do:

- **Define Form Fields:** You specify the fields you need (e.g., text inputs, dropdowns, checkboxes) and their types (e.g., CharField, EmailField, BooleanField).
- **Handle Rendering:** Django can automatically generate the HTML for your form, though you have full control over customization.
- **Validate User Input:** Django performs automatic validation based on the field types and any custom validation rules you define.
- **Clean Data:** Django "cleans" the submitted data, converting it to the correct Python types and handling potential security issues.

Creating Django Forms

You define forms as Python classes that inherit from Django's Form class (or ModelForm for forms that directly relate to your models).

Here's a simple example:

Python

```python
from django import forms
class ContactForm(forms.Form):
    name = forms.CharField(label="Your Name", max_length=100)
    email = forms.EmailField(label="Your Email")
    message = forms.CharField(label="Message", widget=forms.Textarea)
    subscribe = forms.BooleanField(label="Subscribe to newsletter", required=False)
```

In this code:

- We create a ContactForm class.
- Each field is defined as a form field type (e.g., CharField, EmailField).
- label specifies the user-friendly name of the field.
- max_length limits the length of the input.
- widget=forms.Textarea uses a textarea HTML element for the message field.
- required=False makes the "subscribe" field optional.

Rendering Forms in Templates

Django provides several ways to render forms in your HTML templates:

1. **Rendering Fields Manually:** You can render each field individually for maximum control over the HTML structure.

HTML

```
<form method="post">
  {% csrf_token %}
  <div class="form-group">
    {{ form.name.label_tag }}
    {{ form.name }}
    {{ form.name.errors }}
  </div>
  <div class="form-group">
    {{ form.email.label_tag }}
    {{ form.email }}
    {{ form.email.errors }}
  </div>
  <div class="form-group">
    {{ form.message.label_tag }}
    {{ form.message }}
    {{ form.message.errors }}
  </div>
  <button type="submit">Send</button>
</form>
```

- {{ form.name.label_tag }} renders the label for the "name" field.
- {{ form.name }} renders the input field itself.

- {{ form.name.errors }} displays any validation errors for the field.
- {% csrf_token %} is crucial for security; it protects against Cross-Site Request Forgery (CSRF) attacks.

2. **Rendering the Form as a Paragraph:** Django can render the entire form as a series of <p> elements.

HTML

```
<form method="post">
  {% csrf_token %}
  {{ form.as_p }}
  <button type="submit">Send</button>
</form>
```

3. **Rendering the Form as a Table:** Django can render the form inside a table.

HTML

```
<form method="post">
  {% csrf_token %}
  {{ form.as_table }}
  <button type="submit">Send</button>
</form>
```

4. **Rendering the Form as a List:** Django can render the form inside a list.

HTML

```html
<form method="post">
  {% csrf_token %}
  {{ form.as_ul }}
  <button type="submit">Send</button>
</form>
```

Handling Form Submissions

In your view, you'll need to handle the form submission. Here's how:

1. **Display the Form (GET Request):** When the user first accesses the page, you'll typically display an empty form.

Python

```python
from django.shortcuts import render
from .forms import ContactForm
def contact_view(request):
form = ContactForm()
return render(request, 'contact.html', {'form': form})
```

2. **Process the Form (POST Request):** When the user submits the form, you'll process the data.

Python

```python
from django.shortcuts import render, redirect
from .forms import ContactForm
from django.contrib import messages
def contact_view(request):
    if request.method == 'POST':
        form = ContactForm(request.POST)  # Bind the form to the submitted data
        if form.is_valid():
            # Form data is valid, process it
            name = form.cleaned_data['name']
            email = form.cleaned_data['email']
            message = form.cleaned_data['message']
            # Send email or save to database (example)
            # ... your logic here ...
            messages.success(request, "Your message has been sent!")
            return redirect('contact')  # Redirect to the contact page
        else:
            # Form data is invalid, display errors
            return render(request, 'contact.html', {'form': form})
    else:
        form = ContactForm()
        return render(request, 'contact.html', {'form': form})
```

- form = ContactForm(request.POST) creates a form instance and populates it with the submitted data.
- form.is_valid() performs validation.
- form.cleaned_data contains the validated data, converted to Python types.

- messages.success() displays a success message to the user (you'll need to configure Django's messages framework).
- redirect('contact') redirects the user back to the contact page (assuming you have a URL pattern named 'contact').

Form Validation

Django automatically validates form data based on the field types. For example, EmailField ensures the input is a valid email address. You can also add custom validation.

1. **Built-in Validation:** Django provides built-in validation for various field types.
   - CharField and TextField: max_length, min_length, required
   - EmailField: Valid email format
   - URLField: Valid URL format
   - IntegerField: max_value, min_value
2. **Custom Validation:** You can add custom validation logic:
   - **Field-Specific Validation:** Create a method named clean_<field_name> in your form class.

Python

```
from django import forms
from django.core.exceptions import ValidationError
```

```python
class MyForm(forms.Form):
    my_field = forms.CharField()
    def clean_my_field(self):
    data = self.cleaned_data['my_field']
    if len(data) < 5:
        raise ValidationError("My field must be at least 5
characters long.")
    return data
```

- o **Form-Wide Validation:** Create a method named
  clean in your form class. This is useful for
  validation that involves multiple fields.

Python

```python
from django import forms
from django.core.exceptions import ValidationError
class MyForm(forms.Form):
    field1 = forms.CharField()
    field2 = forms.CharField()
    def clean(self):
        cleaned_data = super().clean()
        field1 = cleaned_data.get('field1')
        field2 = cleaned_data.get('field2')
        if field1 == field2:
            raise ValidationError("Field 1 and Field 2 must be
different.")
        return cleaned_data
```

Model Forms

If your form is closely tied to a Django model, you can use ModelForm. It simplifies the process of creating forms that create or update model instances.

Python

```python
from django import forms
from myapp.models import MyModel
class MyModelForm(forms.ModelForm):
    class Meta:
    model = MyModel
     fields = ['field1', 'field2']  # Specify the model fields you want in the form
```

Real-World Examples

- **User Registration:** Collecting username, password, email, etc., and validating their format and uniqueness.
- **Contact Forms:** Gathering user inquiries and validating email addresses.
- **Product Search:** Allowing users to filter products based on keywords, price ranges, etc.
- **Data Entry:** Creating interfaces for administrators to manage data in a database.

Django's form handling and validation features are powerful tools for building robust and user-friendly web applications. They simplify form creation, improve security, and enhance the user experience by providing clear and helpful feedback.

5.5 Working with Sessions and Cookies

The HTTP protocol, which underlies web communication, is inherently stateless. This means that each request from a browser to a server is treated as independent of any previous requests. The server doesn't automatically "remember" who the user is or what they've done on previous pages.

However, most web applications need to maintain some state. Think about:

- **User Logins:** Remembering that a user has logged in and allowing them to access protected pages.
- **Shopping Carts:** Keeping track of the items a user has added to their cart.
- **User Preferences:** Storing settings like language choice or theme selection.

This is where sessions and cookies come into play.

Understanding Cookies

A cookie is a small piece of data that a web server sends to a user's browser. The browser then stores this data and sends it back to the server with subsequent requests. Cookies are stored on the user's computer.

Here's how they work:

1. The server sends an HTTP response with a Set-Cookie header.
2. The browser stores the cookie.
3. For subsequent requests to the same server, the browser includes the cookie in the Cookie header.

Cookies are useful for storing small amounts of data that the server needs to remember about the user. Common uses include:

- **Session Identifiers:** Cookies are often used to store a unique identifier for a user's session (more on sessions below).
- **Preferences:** Storing user preferences like language, theme, or font size.
- **Tracking:** (With privacy implications) Tracking user activity on a website.

Important Considerations for Cookies:

- **Size Limits:** Cookies have size limits (around 4KB).
- **Security:** Cookies can be vulnerable to certain attacks, such as Cross-Site Scripting (XSS). Avoid storing sensitive information directly in cookies.
- **Privacy:** Be mindful of user privacy. Clearly explain your cookie policy and obtain consent where required.

Understanding Sessions

Sessions provide a more robust way to store user-specific data on the server. Instead of storing data directly on the user's browser, the server creates a session for each user and stores the data there. The server then sends a unique session identifier to the user's browser, typically stored in a cookie.

Here's how sessions work in Django:

1. When a user first visits your site, Django creates a new session and stores it in the database (or another storage backend).

2. Django sends the user a cookie containing the session ID.
3. For subsequent requests from the same user, the browser sends the session ID cookie.
4. Django uses the session ID to retrieve the user's session data from the storage backend.

Sessions are generally preferred for storing more sensitive or larger amounts of data because the data itself remains on the server.

Working with Sessions in Django

Django provides built-in session management. You don't need to deal with the complexities of cookie handling directly.

1. **Session Middleware:** Django's session functionality is enabled by default through the SessionMiddleware. Ensure it's present in your MIDDLEWARE setting in settings.py.

Python

```
MIDDLEWARE = [
    # ...
    'django.contrib.sessions.middleware.SessionMiddleware',
    # ...
]
```

2. **Accessing the Session:** In your views, you can access the session data through the request.session attribute, which acts like a dictionary.

Python

```
from django.shortcuts import render
def my_view(request):
  # Access session data
    visits = request.session.get('visits', 0)  # Get 'visits' or
default to 0
  request.session['visits'] = visits + 1   # Increment and set
'visits'
  # Set session data
  request.session['username'] = 'john_doe'
  # Get session data
  username = request.session.get('username')

  # Delete session data
  del request.session['username']
  # Clear the entire session
  request.session.flush()
    return render(request, 'my_template.html', {'visits': visits,
'username': username})
```

   o request.session.get(key, default): Retrieves a session value or returns the default if the key doesn't exist.
   o request.session[key] = value: Sets a session value.

- o del request.session[key]: Deletes a session value.
- o request.session.flush(): Clears all session data.
3. **Session Expiration:** Django sessions have a default expiration time. You can configure this in your settings.py file using the SESSION_COOKIE_AGE setting (in seconds). You can also control whether the session expires when the user closes their browser (SESSION_EXPIRE_AT_BROWSER_CLOSE).

Python

```
SESSION_COOKIE_AGE = 1209600  # 2 weeks
SESSION_EXPIRE_AT_BROWSER_CLOSE = True
```

4. **Session Storage:** Django supports various session storage backends, including:
   - o **Database:** The default, storing session data in your database.
   - o **Cache:** Using your cache system (e.g., Memcached, Redis) for faster access.
   - o **File:** Storing session data in files on the server.
   - o **Cookies:** Storing session data directly in the cookie (not recommended for large or sensitive data).

You can configure the session storage backend using the SESSION_ENGINE setting.

Examples

- **User Authentication:** After a user logs in, you store their user ID in the session to track their logged-in status.
- **Shopping Carts:** You store the items a user has added to their cart in the session.
- **Wizard Forms:** If you have a multi-step form, you can store the user's input from each step in the session until they submit the final form.
- **Rate Limiting:** You can use sessions to track the number of requests a user has made within a certain time period to prevent abuse.

Important Considerations for Sessions:

- **Performance:** Session storage can impact performance, especially if you're using the database backend. Consider using a cache backend for better performance.
- **Security:** Protect your session data. Use HTTPS to encrypt communication and take other security measures.
- **Scalability:** When scaling your application across multiple servers, you need to ensure that session data is shared between the servers.

By understanding how sessions and cookies work in Django, you can build web applications that provide a more personalized and interactive user experience.

Chapter 6: Django REST Framework (DRF)

In this chapter, we'll explore the Django REST Framework (DRF), a fantastic tool for creating powerful and flexible web APIs. We'll cover RESTful principles, setting up DRF, working with serializers, using viewsets and routers, and securing your APIs. Get ready to make your Django applications communicate with the world!

6.1 Introduction to RESTful APIs

First, let's clarify what an API is. API stands for Application Programming Interface. In simple terms, it's a set of rules and protocols that allow[1] different software applications to communicate with each other. Think of it as a[2] contract that defines how different pieces of software can request and exchange information.

Now, REST is an architectural style for designing networked applications. It's a set of principles that, when followed, leads to APIs that are easy to understand, use, and scale.

Key Principles of REST

REST is based on several core principles:

1. **Resource Identification:**
   o In REST, everything is a "resource." A resource can be any piece of information that can be named. Examples include:
     ▪ A user

- A product
- A blog post
  - ○ Each resource is identified by a unique URL (Uniform Resource Locator). For example, the URL /users/123/ might identify the user with ID 123.

Example:

```
# Get information about a specific book
GET /books/978-0321765723
```

2. **Representations:**
   - ○ Resources can have multiple representations. For example, a user's data can be represented as JSON, XML, or HTML.
   - ○ The client (the application making the request) can specify the desired representation using the Accept header in the HTTP request.

Example:

```
# Request data in JSON format
GET /users/123/
Accept: application/json
```

3. **HTTP Methods:**

- REST uses standard HTTP methods to perform operations on resources. The most common methods are:
    - **GET:** Retrieve a resource.
    - **POST:** Create a new resource.
    - **PUT:** Update an existing resource.
    - **DELETE:** Delete a resource.[3]
- **Example:**

```
# Create a new book
POST /books/
Content-Type: application/json
{
  "title": "The Hitchhiker's Guide to the Galaxy",
  "author": "Douglas Adams"
}
# Update a book's title
PUT /books/978-0345391802/
Content-Type: application/json
{
  "title": "The Ultimate Hitchhiker's Guide"
}
# Delete a book
DELETE /books/978-0345391802/
```

-
-

4. **Statelessness:**
    - REST is stateless. This means that each request from a client to a server must contain all the information necessary to understand and

process the request. The server does not store any information about[4] the client's session between requests.

- o This improves scalability because the server doesn't have to manage session data.

5. **HATEOAS (Hypermedia as the Engine of Application State):**
   - o This is an optional but important REST principle. It means that the API should provide links to related resources in its responses. This allows clients to dynamically discover and navigate the API.
   - o **Example:**

JSON

```
# Response to GET /users/123/
{
  "id": 123,
  "username": "john.doe",
  "profile_url": "/users/123/profile/",
  "posts_url": "/users/123/posts/"
}
```

The response includes URLs to the user's profile and posts.

Benefits of RESTful APIs

- **Simplicity:** RESTful APIs are easy to understand and use due to their clear conventions.
- **Scalability:** The stateless nature of REST makes it easy to scale applications.
- **Flexibility:** RESTful APIs can be used with various data formats (JSON, XML) and programming languages.
- **Interoperability:** RESTful APIs promote communication between different systems.

Practical Example: A Simple RESTful API for a To-Do List

Let's illustrate REST concepts with a basic to-do list API:

- **Resources:** tasks
- **Base URL:** /tasks/

Here's how we might interact with this API:

- **GET /tasks/:** Retrieve a list of all tasks.
- **POST /tasks/:** Create a new task. The request body would contain the task details (e.g., title, description).
- **GET /tasks/123/:** Retrieve the task with ID 123.
- **PUT /tasks/123/:** Update the task with ID 123. The request body would contain the updated task details.
- **DELETE /tasks/123/:** Delete the task with ID 123.

This simple example demonstrates how REST uses resources and HTTP methods to perform common operations.

RESTful APIs are a cornerstone of modern web development, enabling communication between web applications, mobile apps, and other systems. By adhering to REST principles, you can build APIs that are efficient, scalable, and easy to use.

6.2 Setting Up DRF

Before we can start building RESTful APIs with Django, we need to install and configure the Django REST Framework. DRF is a third-party package that provides a toolkit for building Web APIs. It's incredibly flexible and provides a lot of functionality out of the box, saving you a significant amount of development time.

1. Installing DRF

The first step is to install DRF using pip, Python's package installer. Open your terminal or command prompt and, make sure your virtual environment is activated, and run the following command:

Bash

```
pip install djangorestframework
```

This command downloads and installs the latest stable version of DRF and its dependencies. Once the installation is complete, you should see a success message.

2. Adding DRF to INSTALLED_APPS

After installing DRF, you need to tell Django that you want to use it in your project. You do this by adding 'rest_framework' to the INSTALLED_APPS list in your project's settings.py file.

Here's how to do it:

1. Open your settings.py file. It's usually located in the inner directory with the same name as your project (e.g., myproject/myproject/settings.py).
2. Find the INSTALLED_APPS list. It's a Python list containing strings, where each string represents the name of a Django app.
3. Add 'rest_framework' to the list. It's good practice to add it towards the end of the list.

Here's an example of how your INSTALLED_APPS might look:

Python

```
INSTALLED_APPS = [
    'django.contrib.admin',
    'django.contrib.auth',
    'django.contrib.contenttypes',
    'django.contrib.sessions',
    'django.contrib.messages',
    'django.contrib.staticfiles',
    'myapp', # Your app
    'rest_framework', # Django REST Framework
]
```

Make sure that the string 'rest_framework' is included in this list.

3. (Optional) Configuring DRF Settings

DRF has various settings that you can customize to control its behavior. While the default settings are often sufficient for getting started, you might want to adjust them for specific requirements.

You can configure DRF settings by creating a REST_FRAMEWORK dictionary in your settings.py file.

Here are a couple of common settings you might want to adjust:

- **DEFAULT_PERMISSION_CLASSES:** This setting controls the default permission classes applied to your API views. By default, DRF allows any request. You might want to restrict access to authenticated users or specific user roles.

Python

```
REST_FRAMEWORK = {
  'DEFAULT_PERMISSION_CLASSES': [

'rest_framework.permissions.IsAuthenticatedOrReadOnly',
  ]
}
```

This example sets the default permission class to IsAuthenticatedOrReadOnly, which means that any authenticated user can access the API, but only authenticated users can create, update, or delete resources.

- **DEFAULT_AUTHENTICATION_CLASSES:** This setting controls the default authentication classes used to authenticate requests. DRF supports various authentication schemes, such as Basic Authentication, Session Authentication, and Token Authentication.

Python

```python
REST_FRAMEWORK = {
  'DEFAULT_AUTHENTICATION_CLASSES': [
    'rest_framework.authentication.SessionAuthentication',
    'rest_framework.authentication.BasicAuthentication',
    'rest_framework.authentication.TokenAuthentication',
  ]
}
```

This example enables Session Authentication, Basic Authentication, and Token Authentication.

These are just a few examples of DRF settings. You can find a comprehensive list of available settings in the DRF documentation.

Practical Example: Verifying the Setup

To verify that DRF is installed and configured correctly, you can run your Django development server and try accessing the DRF API root.

1. Run the development server:

Bash

```
python manage.py runserver
```

2. Open your browser and navigate to http://127.0.0.1:8000/.

If DRF is set up correctly, you should see a basic API root view. This view is automatically generated by DRF and lists the available API endpoints.

Real-World Application

Setting up DRF is the foundational step for building any API with Django. Whether you're creating a mobile app backend, integrating with other services, or building a public API, a correctly configured DRF environment is essential.

By following these steps, you've successfully installed and configured Django REST Framework in your Django project. You're now ready to start defining your API endpoints, serializing data, and handling requests.

6.3 Serializers and Deserializers

In a web API, data is typically exchanged in formats like JSON. However, your Django application works with Python objects, such as model instances. Serializers and deserializers act as the bridge between these two worlds.

Understanding Serializers

A serializer takes complex data, such as Django model instances, and converts it into a format that can be easily rendered into JSON, XML, or other output formats. This process is called *serialization*.

Think of a serializer as a translator. It takes your Python objects and turns them into a format that a client application (like a web browser or a mobile app) can understand.

Here's why serializers are essential:

- **Data Transformation:** They ensure that your data is in the correct format for the API's consumers.
- **Data Filtering:** They allow you to control which data is included in the API response. You might not want to expose all fields of your model.
- **Data Formatting:** They can format data, such as dates or numbers, according to the API's requirements.

Understanding Deserializers

A deserializer does the opposite of a serializer. It takes data from an incoming request (e.g., JSON data sent by a client) and converts it back into Python data types, typically Django model instances. This process is called *deserialization*.

Deserializers are crucial for:

- **Data Validation:** They can validate the incoming data to ensure it meets your application's requirements.
- **Data Conversion:** They convert the incoming data into the correct Python types.

- **Object Creation/Update:** They can be used to create new model instances or update existing ones based on the incoming data.

Creating Serializers

In DRF, you create serializers by defining classes that inherit from rest_framework.serializers.Serializer or, more commonly, rest_framework.serializers.ModelSerializer. ModelSerializer provides a shortcut for creating serializers that work directly with Django models.

Here's an example of a ModelSerializer:

Python

```python
from rest_framework import serializers
from myapp.models import Product
class ProductSerializer(serializers.ModelSerializer):
    class Meta:
        model = Product
        fields = ['id', 'name', 'description', 'price']
```

In this code:

- We create a ProductSerializer that is associated with the Product model.
- The fields list specifies which model fields should be included in the serialized output.

Serializer Fields

Serializers use serializer fields to define how each piece of data should be handled. DRF provides a wide range of field types, similar to Django model fields:

- CharField: For strings.
- IntegerField: For integers.
- FloatField: For floating-point numbers.
- DecimalField: For decimal numbers.
- BooleanField: For boolean values.
- DateTimeField: For dates and times.
- PrimaryKeyRelatedField: For relationships with other models.

You can also customize serializer fields with various options, such as:

- read_only=True: The field is included in the output but not used for input.
- write_only=True: The field is used for input but not included in the output.
- required=True: The field is required for input.
- max_length: The maximum length for character fields.

Using Serializers

Here's how you can use serializers to serialize and deserialize data:

1. **Serializing Data:**

Python

from myapp.models import Product

```python
from myapp.serializers import ProductSerializer
# Get a product instance
product = Product.objects.get(pk=1)
# Serialize the product
serializer = ProductSerializer(product)
serialized_data = serializer.data   # This is a Python
dictionary
print(serialized_data)
```

This code retrieves a Product object and serializes it into a Python dictionary. DRF can then render this dictionary into JSON.

2. **Deserializing Data:**

Python

```python
from myapp.serializers import ProductSerializer
# Incoming data (e.g., from a request)
data = {'name': 'New Product', 'description': 'A great
product', 'price': 99.99}
# Deserialize the data
serializer = ProductSerializer(data=data)
if serializer.is_valid():
    validated_data = serializer.validated_data
    # Create a new product instance
    product = Product.objects.create(**validated_data)
    print("Product created:", product)
else:
    print("Validation errors:", serializer.errors)
```

This code takes incoming data (simulated here as a dictionary), deserializes it, validates it, and creates a new Product object if the data is valid.

Real-World Examples

- **E-commerce API:** Serializers would be used to present product details (name, price, description) to a mobile app or website. Deserializers would be used to create new products or update existing ones through an admin interface.
- **Social Media API:** Serializers would format user profiles, posts, and comments for display. Deserializers would handle creating new posts or updating profile information.
- **Data Analytics API:** Serializers would convert data from a database into a format suitable for analysis or visualization. Deserializers might be used to receive data from external sources and store it in the database.

Serializers and deserializers are the backbone of data handling in DRF. They enable you to work with your Django models and other data in a way that's efficient and compatible with the needs of your API.

6.4 ViewSets and Routers

When building an API, you'll often need to perform a set of common operations on your resources (like creating, retrieving, updating, and deleting objects). DRF's ViewSets and Routers simplify this process, reducing boilerplate code and making your API code more organized.

Understanding ViewSets

A ViewSet is a class that provides the implementation for a set of related views. It combines the logic for handling multiple actions on a resource into a single class.

DRF provides several base ViewSet classes that you can inherit from:

- ViewSet: The base class. You'll need to define all the actions yourself.
- ReadOnlyModelViewSet: Provides read-only operations (list and retrieve).
- ModelViewSet: Provides complete CRUD (Create, Retrieve, Update, Delete) operations.

Here are the common actions that a ViewSet can handle:

- list: Retrieve a list of resources.
- retrieve: Retrieve a single resource.
- create: Create a new resource.
- update: Update an existing resource.
- partial_update: Partially update an existing resource.
- destroy: Delete a resource.

Here's an example of a ModelViewSet:

Python

from rest_framework import viewsets

```python
from myapp.models import Product
from myapp.serializers import ProductSerializer
class ProductViewSet(viewsets.ModelViewSet):
    queryset = Product.objects.all()
    serializer_class = ProductSerializer
```

In this code:

- We create a ProductViewSet that inherits from ModelViewSet.
- queryset = Product.objects.all(): This tells the ViewSet which objects to use for its operations.
- serializer_class = ProductSerializer: This specifies the serializer to use for converting data.

By using ModelViewSet, we get all the standard API actions (list, retrieve, create, update, delete) for free.

Understanding Routers

Routers are classes that automatically generate the URL patterns for your ViewSets. They simplify the process of mapping URLs to your API views, saving you from writing repetitive URL configurations.

DRF provides several router classes:

- SimpleRouter: Generates basic URL patterns.
- DefaultRouter: Generates more comprehensive URL patterns, including a root view with a list of available API endpoints.

Here's how to use a DefaultRouter:

Python

```
from rest_framework import routers
from myapp.views import ProductViewSet
router = routers.DefaultRouter()
router.register(r'products', ProductViewSet) # r'products' is
the base URL for this ViewSet
urlpatterns = router.urls
```

In this code:

- We create a DefaultRouter.
- router.register(r'products', ProductViewSet): This registers the ProductViewSet with the router, specifying that the base URL for this ViewSet should be /products/.
- urlpatterns = router.urls: This gets the list of generated URL patterns from the router and includes them in your project's urlpatterns.

The DefaultRouter will automatically generate the following URLs:

- GET /products/: List all products.
- POST /products/: Create a new product.
- GET /products/{id}/: Retrieve the product with the given ID.
- PUT /products/{id}/: Update the product with the given ID.
- PATCH /products/{id}/: Partially update the product with the given ID.
- DELETE /products/{id}/: Delete the product with the given ID.

Benefits of Using ViewSets and Routers

- **Reduced Code:** ViewSets and Routers significantly reduce the amount of code you need to write for common API patterns.
- **Improved Organization:** They help you structure your API views and URLs in a clear and consistent way.
- **Consistency:** They enforce consistent URL conventions and API behavior.
- **Rapid Development:** They speed up the development process by automating common tasks.

Practical Example: Building a Simple Product API

Let's put ViewSets and Routers together to build a simple API for managing products.

1. **Define Model and Serializer:**

Python

```
# myapp/models.py
from django.db import models
class Product(models.Model):
    name = models.CharField(max_length=200)
    description = models.TextField()
    price = models.DecimalField(max_digits=10, decimal_places=2)
    def __str__(self):
    return self.name
# myapp/serializers.py
from rest_framework import serializers
```

```python
from .models import Product
class ProductSerializer(serializers.ModelSerializer):
    class Meta:
        model = Product
        fields = '__all__'
```

2. **Create ViewSet:**

Python

```python
# myapp/views.py
from rest_framework import viewsets
from .models import Product
from .serializers import ProductSerializer
class ProductViewSet(viewsets.ModelViewSet):
    queryset = Product.objects.all()
    serializer_class = ProductSerializer
```

3. **Register ViewSet with Router:**

Python

```python
# myproject/urls.py
from django.urls import path, include
from rest_framework import routers
from myapp import views
router = routers.DefaultRouter()
router.register(r'products', views.ProductViewSet)
urlpatterns = [
```

```
    path('admin/', admin.site.urls),
    path('api/', include(router.urls)),
]
```

Now, you have a fully functional API for managing products with just a few lines of code!

Real-World Applications

- **E-commerce APIs:** Managing products, orders, customers, etc.
- **Social Media APIs:** Managing users, posts, comments, etc.
- **Content Management Systems (CMS) APIs:** Managing articles, pages, media, etc.

ViewSets and Routers are powerful tools that simplify API development in Django REST Framework. By using them effectively, you can build clean, efficient, and maintainable APIs.

6.5 Authentication and Permissions in DRF

When building an API, you need to answer two key questions:

1. **Authentication:** Who is making this request?
2. **Permissions:** Is this user allowed to perform this action?

DRF provides a flexible and powerful system for handling both authentication and permissions.

Understanding Authentication

Authentication is the process of verifying the identity of a user or client making a request. DRF supports various authentication schemes:

- **Basic Authentication:**
  - A simple scheme where the client sends the username and password in the Authorization header, encoded in Base64.
  - Not recommended for production due to security concerns (password is easily decoded).
  - Useful for testing.
- **Session Authentication:**
  - Uses Django's built-in session management.
  - Suitable for APIs that are accessed by a web browser that also uses Django's session system.
- **Token Authentication:**
  - Uses a unique token string for authentication.
  - More secure than Basic Authentication.
  - Commonly used for APIs accessed by mobile apps or other systems.

Practical Implementation: Setting Up Token Authentication

Let's walk through how to set up Token Authentication.

1. **Install DRF's Token Authentication:**
2. DRF's Token Authentication is included in the rest_framework.authtoken app. You need to add it to your INSTALLED_APPS in settings.py:

Python

```
INSTALLED_APPS = [
    # ...
    'rest_framework',
    'rest_framework.authtoken', # Add this line
    # ...
]
```

3. **Run Migrations:**

   You need to create the database tables for the token system:

Bash

```
python manage.py migrate
```

4. **Configure Default Authentication Classes:**

   In your settings.py, set the DEFAULT_AUTHENTICATION_CLASSES setting to use TokenAuthentication:

Python

```
REST_FRAMEWORK = {
```

```
'DEFAULT_AUTHENTICATION_CLASSES': [
'rest_framework.authentication.TokenAuthentication',
]
}
```

5. **Obtain Tokens:**

   DRF provides a view that allows users to obtain their tokens. You need to include the rest_framework.urls in your project's urls.py:

Python

```
from django.urls import path, include
from rest_framework import routers
router = routers.DefaultRouter()
# ... register your viewsets here ...
urlpatterns = [
    path('api-auth/', include('rest_framework.urls')),  # Add this line
    path('api/', include(router.urls)),
]
```

You can now get the token by making a POST request to the /api-token-auth/ endpoint.

6. **Create Tokens for Users:**

   You can create tokens for users in several ways:

- **Signal:** Automatically create a token when a user is created.

Python

```
from django.conf import settings
from django.db.models.signals import post_save
from django.dispatch import receiver
from rest_framework.authtoken.models import Token
@receiver(post_save, sender=settings.AUTH_USER_MODEL)
def create_auth_token(sender, instance=None, created=False, **kwargs):
    if created:
    Token.objects.create(user=instance)
```

- **Admin**[1] **Interface:** You can create tokens manually in the Django admin interface.
- **Programmatically:** You can create tokens in your code.

Python

```
from rest_framework.authtoken.models import Token
from django.contrib.auth.models import User
user = User.objects.get(username='myuser')
token, created = Token.objects.get_or_create(user=user)
```

```
print(token.key)
```

7. **Include the Token in Requests:**

Clients need to include the token in the Authorization header of their requests:

```
Authorization:                              Token
9944b099c67c1d80be8ac04c2b45e2979681b7f0
```

Understanding Permissions

Permissions control *access* to your API endpoints. They determine whether an authenticated user is *authorized* to perform a specific action. DRF provides several built-in permission classes:

- AllowAny: Allows access to all users, authenticated or not.
- IsAuthenticated: Allows access only to authenticated users.
- IsAdminUser: Allows access only to admin users.
- IsAuthenticatedOrReadOnly: Allows read–only access to unauthenticated users, but write access only to authenticated users.
- DjangoModelPermissions: Uses Django's standard model permissions to control access.
- DjangoObjectPermissions: Uses Django's object-level permissions to control access to individual objects.

Practical Implementation: Setting Up Permissions

You can set permissions at the view level:

Python

```
from rest_framework import viewsets, permissions
from myapp.models import Product
from myapp.serializers import ProductSerializer
class ProductViewSet(viewsets.ModelViewSet):
    queryset = Product.objects.all()
    serializer_class = ProductSerializer
                                    permission_classes        =
[permissions.IsAuthenticatedOrReadOnly]
```

This code allows anyone to read product data (GET requests), but only authenticated users can create, update, or delete products (POST, PUT, DELETE requests).

Combining Authentication and Permissions

Authentication and permissions work together. A user must first be authenticated, and then their permissions are checked to determine if they are allowed to proceed.

Real-World Examples

- **E-commerce API:**
    - Authentication: Using Token Authentication to allow mobile apps to access the API.
    - Permissions: Allowing only administrators to create or update products, while customers can only view product details and place orders.
- **Social Media API:**
    - Authentication: Using OAuth2 to allow third-party applications to access user data.

- Permissions: Allowing users to only view their own profile information, while moderators can delete inappropriate posts.

By carefully implementing authentication and permissions, you can secure your APIs and protect your valuable data.

6.6 API Documentation using Swagger or Redoc

When you build an API, you're not just creating code; you're creating a tool for other developers. To make that tool useful, you need to provide clear and comprehensive documentation. Documentation should explain:

- What endpoints are available.
- What HTTP methods to use for each endpoint.
- What data formats to send and receive.
- What authentication methods are required.
- What errors to expect.

Manually writing and maintaining API documentation can be tedious and error-prone. Fortunately, there are tools that can automatically generate documentation from your API code. Swagger and Redoc are two popular options.

Understanding Swagger (OpenAPI)

Swagger (now known as the OpenAPI Specification) is a widely used standard for describing RESTful APIs. It provides a language-agnostic format for documenting API structure, including:

- Endpoints and operations (GET, POST, etc.)
- Request and response parameters
- Data types
- Authentication methods

Tools can then use this specification to generate interactive documentation, client libraries, and server stubs.

Using Swagger with Django REST Framework

To use Swagger with DRF, you'll typically use a library like drf-yasg (Django REST Framework Yet Another Swagger Generator).

Here's a general outline of how to set it up:

1. **Install** drf-yasg:

Bash

```
pip install drf-yasg
```

2. **Add** drf-yasg **to** INSTALLED_APPS:

Python

```
INSTALLED_APPS = [
    # ...
```

```python
    'rest_framework',
    'drf_yasg',
    # ...
]
```

3. **Configure URL Patterns:**

   You need to add URL patterns that will serve the generated Swagger/OpenAPI schema and the Swagger UI.

Python

```python
from django.urls import path, re_path
from rest_framework import permissions
from drf_yasg.views import get_schema_view
from drf_yasg import openapi
schema_view = get_schema_view(
    openapi.Info(
        title="Your API",
        default_version='v1',
        description="A description of your API",
        terms_of_service="https://www.example.com/terms/",

contact=openapi.Contact(email="contact@example.com"),
        license=openapi.License(name="BSD License"),
    ),
    public=True,
    permission_classes=(permissions.AllowAny,),
)
```

```
urlpatterns = [
    # ... your other URL patterns ...
                                    path('swagger<format>/',
schema_view.without_ui(cache_timeout=0),
name='schema-json'),
        path('swagger/',  schema_view.with_ui('swagger',
cache_timeout=0), name='schema-swagger-ui'),
            path('redoc/',    schema_view.with_ui('redoc',
cache_timeout=0), name='schema-redoc'),
]
```

- o get_schema_view():[1] This function generates the OpenAPI schema. You can customize the API information using the openapi.Info object.
- o schema_view.without_ui(): This serves the raw OpenAPI schema (in JSON or YAML format).
- o schema_view.with_ui('swagger'): This serves the Swagger UI, an interactive documentation interface.
- o schema_view.with_ui('redoc'): This serves the Redoc UI, another documentation interface.

4. **Run Your Server and Access the Documentation:**

Start your Django development server and visit the URLs you configured (e.g., http://127.0.0.1:8000/swagger/ or http://127.0.0.1:8000/redoc/) to view the generated documentation.

Understanding Redoc

Redoc is another tool for generating API documentation from OpenAPI specifications. It focuses on providing a clean and readable documentation experience. Redoc often produces documentation that is more visually appealing than Swagger UI.

Choosing Between Swagger and Redoc

Both Swagger and Redoc are excellent tools. The choice between them often comes down to personal preference and specific requirements.

- **Swagger UI:** Provides an interactive interface that allows you to test API endpoints directly from the documentation.
- **Redoc:** Emphasizes a clean and readable layout, often preferred for public-facing APIs.

Documenting Your API Effectively

Regardless of the tool you choose, here are some best practices for documenting your API:

- **Be Clear and Concise:** Use clear and simple language. Avoid jargon.
- **Provide Examples:** Include example requests and responses to illustrate how to use each endpoint.
- **Document All Parameters:** Clearly describe each request parameter, including its data type, whether it's required, and any validation rules.
- **Document Response Codes:** Explain the meaning of each HTTP response code (e.g., 200 OK, 400 Bad Request, 500 Internal Server Error).

- **Use Consistent Formatting:** Maintain a consistent style and formatting throughout your documentation.

Example

Consider an e-commerce API. Good documentation would be essential for developers who want to integrate with your platform to:

- Retrieve product information.
- Place orders.
- Manage inventory.

Clear and accurate documentation would enable these developers to quickly and easily build integrations, leading to a more successful and widely adopted API.

By using tools like Swagger or Redoc and following best practices, you can create API documentation that is both helpful and professional. This will significantly improve the developer experience and contribute to the success of your API.

Chapter 7: Django Templates and Static Files

Let's learn how to make our Django applications look beautiful and interactive! In this chapter, we'll cover Django templates, which allow you to create dynamic HTML, and static files, which include your CSS, JavaScript, and images. We'll learn about template syntax, inheritance, static file management, and template tags and filters. Get ready to build engaging user interfaces!

7.1 Template Syntax and Variables

Django's template language provides a way to create dynamic HTML. This means that instead of just static HTML that always displays the same content, you can generate HTML that changes based on the data your application is working with.

The core of this dynamic behavior comes from template syntax, which allows you to embed variables and logic within your HTML files.

Understanding Variables

Variables are how you display data from your Django views in your templates. When a view processes a request and renders a template, it can pass data to the template in a "context." You then access this data using variables within the template.

Variables are enclosed in double curly braces: {{ variable_name }}

Here's a simple example:

Let's say you have a view that looks like this:

Python

```python
from django.shortcuts import render
def my_view(request):
    context = {
    'message': 'Hello, Django!',
    'user_name': 'Alice',
    }
    return render(request, 'my_template.html', context)
```

In this view:

- We create a dictionary called context. This dictionary holds the data we want to pass to the template.
- The keys of the dictionary ('message', 'user_name') become the variable names you use in the template.
- We use render() to combine the template my_template.html with the context data.

Now, in your my_template.html file, you can use these variables:

HTML

```html
<!DOCTYPE html>
<html>
<head>
  <title>My Template</title>
</head>
```

```
<body>
  <h1>{{ message }}</h1>
  <p>Welcome, {{ user_name }}!</p>
</body>
</html>
```

When this template is rendered, Django will replace {{ message }} with the string 'Hello, Django!' and {{ user_name }} with the string 'Alice'. The resulting HTML sent to the browser will be:

HTML

```
<!DOCTYPE html>
<html>
<head>
  <title>My Template</title>
</head>
<body>
  <h1>Hello, Django!</h1>
  <p>Welcome, Alice!</p>
</body>
</html>
```

Variable Lookup Rules

When Django encounters a variable in a template, it follows a specific lookup order to find the value:

1. **Dictionary Lookup:** If the variable is a dictionary key, Django tries to find the value associated with that key.

2. **Attribute Lookup:** If the variable is an object, Django tries to access an attribute with that name. This includes methods.
3. **List-Index Lookup:** If the variable is a list, Django tries to access an element at that index.

Example with Objects and Methods

Let's say you have a Django model like this:

Python

```
from django.db import models
class Product(models.Model):
    name = models.CharField(max_length=200)
            price   =   models.DecimalField(max_digits=10,
decimal_places=2)
    def discounted_price(self):
    return self.price * 0.9
```

And you pass an instance of this model to your template:

Python

```
from django.shortcuts import render
def product_view(request):
    product = Product.objects.get(pk=1)  # Get the product
with ID 1
        return   render(request,   'product_template.html',
{'product': product})
```

You can access the model's attributes and methods in the template:

HTML

```
<!DOCTYPE html>
<html>
<head>
  <title>{{ product.name }}</title>
</head>
<body>
  <h1>{{ product.name }}</h1>
  <p>Price: ${{ product.price }}</p>
  <p>Discounted Price: ${{ product.discounted_price }}</p>
</body>
</html>
```

Important Notes

- **Dot Notation:** You use dot notation (.) to access attributes and methods of objects.
- **Method Calls:** When you call a method in a template (like {{ product.discounted_price }}), you don't include parentheses.
- **Security:** Django's template language is designed to be secure. It automatically escapes HTML characters in variables to prevent Cross-Site Scripting (XSS) attacks.

Real-World Example

Consider an e-commerce website. A product detail page would use variables to display the product's name, description, price, and other information. The data for these variables would come from the database, fetched by a Django view, and then passed to the template for rendering.

By understanding how to use variables in Django templates, you can create dynamic web pages that display information effectively and interact with your application's data.

7.2 Template Inheritance and Inclusion

When you build a web application, you'll often have pages that share a common structure. Think about a typical website: it might have a header, a navigation menu, a footer, and then the unique content of each page in the middle.

Template inheritance and inclusion are Django's ways of helping you manage this shared structure.

Template Inheritance

Template inheritance allows you to create a "base" template that defines the overall structure of your pages. Then, you can create "child" templates that inherit from the base template and override specific parts of it.

Think of it like a blueprint for your web pages. The base template is the blueprint, and the child templates are variations on that blueprint.

Here's how it works:

1. **Base Template:**
   - The base template contains the common elements of your pages, such as the HTML structure, header, navigation, and footer.

- It uses special template tags called {% block %} to define "blocks" that can be overridden by child templates. Blocks are placeholders for content.
2. Here's an example of a base template (base.html):

HTML

```
<!DOCTYPE html>
<html>
<head>
    <title>{% block title %}My Website{% endblock %}</title>
  <link rel="stylesheet" href="{% static 'style.css' %}">
</head>
<body>
  <div id="header">
    {% block header %}
    <h1>Welcome to My Website</h1>
    <nav>
    <a href="/">Home</a> | <a href="/about/">About</a>
    </nav>
    {% endblock %}
  </div>

  <div id="content">
    {% block content %}
      <p>This is the default content.</p>
    {% endblock %}
  </div>
```

```html
<div id="footer">
  {% block footer %}
    <p>&copy; 2024 My Website</p>
  {% endblock %}
</div>
</body>
</html>
```

- {% block title %}: This defines a block named "title." Child templates can override this to set the page-specific title. The text "My Website" is the default content, used if a child template doesn't override the block.
- {% block header %}, {% block content %}, {% block footer %}: These define blocks for the header, main content, and footer, respectively.
- {% static 'style.css' %}: This is a template tag for including static files (we'll cover this later).

3. **Child Template:**
   - Child templates inherit from the base template using the {% extends %} tag.
   - They then override the blocks defined in the base template to provide the specific content for that page.
4. Here's an example of a child template (about.html) that inherits from base.html:

HTML

```
{% extends 'base.html' %}
{% block title %}About Us{% endblock %}
{% block content %}
  <h2>About Our Company</h2>
  <p>We are a great company...</p>
{% endblock %}
```

- {% extends 'base.html' %}: This tag tells Django that this template inherits from base.html.
- {% block title %}About Us{% endblock %}: This overrides the "title" block from the base template, setting the page title to "About Us."
- {% block content %} ... {% endblock %}: This overrides the "content" block, providing the specific content for the about page.

When Django renders about.html, it first loads base.html and then inserts the content from about.html into the appropriate blocks. The resulting HTML sent to the browser would be:

HTML

```
<!DOCTYPE html>
<html>
<head>
  <title>About Us</title>
  <link rel="stylesheet" href="/static/style.css">
</head>
<body>
```

```
<div id="header">
  <h1>Welcome to My Website</h1>
  <nav>
  <a href="/">Home</a> | <a href="/about/">About</a>
  </nav>
  </div>
  <div id="content">
  <h2>About Our Company</h2>
  <p>We are a great company...</p>
  </div>
  <div id="footer">
  <p>&copy; 2024 My Website</p>
  </div>
</body>
</html>
```

Template Inclusion

Template inclusion allows you to include smaller template snippets within larger templates. This is useful for reusing components like headers, footers, navigation menus, or forms.

You use the `{% include %}` tag to include another template.

Here's an example:

Let's say you have a template called `navigation.html`:

```html
<nav>
```

```
                    <a   href="/">Home</a>   |   <a
href="/products/">Products</a>            |            <a
href="/contact/">Contact</a>
  </nav>
```

You can include this in other templates:

HTML

```
<!DOCTYPE html>
<html>
<head>
  <title>My Page</title>
</head>
<body>
  <div id="header">
  <h1>My Page</h1>
  {% include 'navigation.html' %}
  </div>

  <div id="content">
  <p>Page content...</p>
  </div>
</body>
</html>
```

When Django renders this template, it will insert the contents of navigation.html where the {% include %} tag is.

Practical Examples

- **E-commerce Website:**

- Template inheritance: You could have a base template for all product pages, with blocks for product details, reviews, and related products.
- Template inclusion: You could include a template for the product search bar on multiple pages.
- **Blog:**
  - Template inheritance: You could have a base template for all blog posts, with blocks for the post title, content, author information, and comments.
  - Template inclusion: You could include a template for the sidebar, which displays recent posts and categories.

By using template inheritance and inclusion effectively, you can create more organized, efficient, and maintainable Django templates.

7.3 Working with Static Files (CSS, JavaScript, Images)

When you build a web application, you don't just use HTML. You'll likely want to style your pages with CSS, add interactivity with JavaScript, and display images. These are static files: files that the server serves to the user's browser without any modification.

Django provides a structured way to manage and serve static files, which is important for both development and production environments.

Why Proper Static File Management is Important

- **Organization:** It keeps your project directory clean and organized.
- **Performance:** Django can efficiently serve static files.
- **Flexibility:** It allows you to easily switch between different storage locations for your static files (e.g., local file system vs. a CDN).
- **Security:** It helps prevent accidental exposure of sensitive files.

Setting Up Static Files in Django

Here's how to configure Django to work with static files:

1. **Create a static Directory:**
   - Inside each of your Django apps, create a directory named static.
   - Inside the static directory, it's a good practice to create another directory with the same name as your app. This helps avoid naming conflicts if you have static files with the same name in different apps.
   - For example, if your app is named myapp, your directory structure would look like this:

myapp/
static/

```
myapp/
css/
style.css
js/
script.js
images/
logo.png
```

2. **Configure** settings.py:
   - In your project's settings.py file, make sure that the STATIC_URL setting is defined. It's usually set to /static/ by default. This is the base URL for your static files.

Python

STATIC_URL = '/static/'

   - If you want to collect all your static files into a single directory for deployment (which is recommended for production), you'll also need to configure STATIC_ROOT. This is the absolute path to the directory where collectstatic will gather all your static files.

Python

```
import os
from pathlib import Path
BASE_DIR = Path(__file__).resolve().parent.parent
STATIC_URL = '/static/'
STATIC_ROOT = os.path.join(BASE_DIR, 'staticfiles')
```

- **BASE_DIR**: This variable is usually defined by Django to point to your project's root directory.
- os.path.join(): This function ensures that the path is constructed correctly for your operating system.

3. **Load the** static **Template Tag:**
   - In your templates, you need to load the static template tag set to access your static files. You do this by adding {% load static %} at the top of your template file.

HTML

```
{% load static %}
<!DOCTYPE html>
<html>
<head>
  <title>My Page</title>
        <link rel="stylesheet" href="{% static 'myapp/css/style.css' %}">
  <script src="{% static 'myapp/js/script.js' %}"></script>
</head>
```

```
<body>
    <img src="{% static 'myapp/images/logo.png' %}"
alt="Logo">
  <h1>Welcome!</h1>
  <p>This is my page.</p>
</body>
</html>
```

- {% load static %}: This loads the static template tag set.
- {% static 'myapp/css/style.css' %}: This generates the correct URL for your static file. Django will use the STATIC_URL setting to build the complete URL.

4. **Collecting Static Files (for production):**
   - When you deploy your Django application to a production server, you'll typically want to collect all your static files into a single directory so that your web server can serve them efficiently.
   - To do this, run the collectstatic management command:

Bash

python manage.py collectstatic

   - This command will copy all your static files from your app's static directories (and any other locations configured in STATICFILES_DIRS) to the STATIC_ROOT directory.

Important Considerations

- **STATICFILES_DIRS**: If you have static files that are not tied to a specific app (e.g., project-wide CSS or JavaScript), you can specify additional directories to search for static files in the STATICFILES_DIRS setting in settings.py.

Python

```
STATICFILES_DIRS = [
    os.path.join(BASE_DIR, 'my_project_static'),
]
```

- **Serving Static Files in Development:** Django's development server can serve static files automatically. However, this is *not* recommended for production. In production, you should configure your web server (e.g., Nginx, Apache) to serve static files.
- **Caching:** For production environments, it's essential to configure caching for your static files to improve performance. This can be done through your web server.

Real-World Examples

- **E-commerce Website:**

- CSS files to style the layout, colors, and fonts of the product pages, shopping cart, and checkout process.
  - JavaScript files to handle interactive elements like image galleries, product filtering, and form validation.
  - Image files for product photos, logos, and banners.
- **Social Media Platform:**
  - CSS files to style user profiles, news feeds, and messaging interfaces.
  - JavaScript files to handle real-time updates, notifications, and interactive posts.
  - Image files for user avatars, post attachments, and platform branding.

By following these guidelines, you can effectively manage and serve static files in your Django projects, resulting in well-organized, performant, and visually appealing web applications.

7.4 Template Filters and Tags

Django's template language isn't just about displaying variables. It also provides ways to modify those variables and perform logic within your templates. This is where filters and tags come in.

Understanding Template Filters

Filters are used to modify the output of variables. They are applied using a pipe character (|).

Here's the basic syntax:

HTML

{{ variable | filter_name | another_filter }}

You can chain multiple filters together, and they are applied from left to right.

Django comes with many built-in filters. Here are some common ones:

- lower: Converts a string to lowercase.

HTML

{{ "HELLO" | lower }} {# Output: hello #}

- upper: Converts a string to uppercase.

HTML

{{ "hello" | upper }} {# Output: HELLO #}

- title: Converts a string to title case (first letter of each word capitalized).

HTML

{{ "hello world" | title }} {# Output: Hello World #}

- **truncatechars**: Truncates a string to a specified number of characters. If the string is longer than the specified length, it will be truncated, and a trailing ellipsis (...) will be added.

HTML

{{ "This is a long sentence." | truncatechars:10 }} {# Output: This is a... #}

- **date**: Formats a date object according to a specified format.

HTML

{{ my_date | date:"F j, Y" }} {# Output: January 1, 2024 (if my_date is that date) #}

- **default**: Provides a default value if a variable is Falsey (e.g., None, empty string, 0).

HTML

{{ my_variable | default:"No value provided" }}

- length: Returns the length of a string or list.

HTML

{{ my_list | length }} {# Output: The number of items in my_list #}

Understanding Template Tags

Tags are more complex than filters. They provide control structures and perform actions. Tags are enclosed in curly braces and percent signs: {% tag_name %}

Here are some common tags:

- {% if %}, {% elif %}, {% else %}, {% endif %}: These tags allow you to create conditional statements.

HTML

```
{% if user.is_authenticated %}
   <p>Welcome, {{ user.username }}!</p>
{% else %}
   <p>Please log in.</p>
{% endif %}
```

- {% for %}, {% empty %}, {% endfor %}: These tags allow you to loop through a sequence (e.g., a list).

HTML

```
<ul>
  {% for item in my_list %}
    <li>{{ item }}</li>
  {% empty %}
    <li>No items found.</li>
  {% endfor %}
</ul>
```

- o **The** {% empty %} block is executed if the list is empty.
- {% csrf_token %}: This tag is crucial for security. It generates a token that protects against Cross-Site Request Forgery (CSRF) attacks in forms. You should always include this tag in any form that submits data using the POST method.

HTML

```
<form method="post">
  {% csrf_token %}
  {# ... form fields ... #}
</form>
```

- {% url %}: This tag allows you to generate URLs based on the names you give to your URL patterns in urls.py. This is highly recommended because it makes your templates more robust to URL changes.

Python

```python
# urls.py
from django.urls import path
from . import views
urlpatterns = [
    path('about/', views.about_view, name='about'),
                            path('product/<int:product_id>/',
views.product_detail_view, name='product_detail'),
]
```

HTML

```html
<a href="{% url 'about' %}">About Us</a>
<a href="{% url 'product_detail' product.id %}">{{ product.name }}</a>
```

- {% include %}: This tag allows you to include another template within the current template.

HTML

```html
{% include 'header.html' %}
<p>Main content...</p>
{% include 'footer.html' %}
```

- {% extends %}, {% block %}, {% endblock %}: These tags are used for template inheritance (as discussed in the previous section).

Creating Custom Filters and Tags

You can also create your own custom filters and tags to extend the functionality of the template language. This involves writing Python code and registering your filters and tags with Django.

Real-World Examples

- **Blog:**
  - Filters: Formatting dates of blog posts, truncating long excerpts, converting Markdown to HTML.
  - Tags: Displaying a list of recent posts, generating pagination links, displaying comment forms.
- **E-commerce Website:**
  - Filters: Formatting prices, displaying product availability, converting product descriptions.
  - Tags: Displaying product categories, adding items to the shopping cart, showing user order history.

By mastering template filters and tags, you can create dynamic and interactive web pages with Django, efficiently manipulating data and controlling the presentation of your content.

7.5 Building Dynamic HTML with Django Templates

The power of Django templates lies in their ability to generate HTML that changes based on the data and logic of your application. This is what we mean by "dynamic HTML." It's the opposite of static HTML, which is the same for every user and every visit to a page.

Here's how Django templates help you achieve dynamic HTML:

1. **Displaying Data from Views:**
   ○ As we discussed earlier, you pass data from your Django views to your templates using a context (a Python dictionary).
   ○ The template then uses variables ({{ variable }}) to display that data.

   Example:

Python

```
from django.shortcuts import render

def product_detail_view(request, product_id):
product = Product.objects.get(pk=product_id)
return render(request, 'product_detail.html', {'product':
product})
```

HTML

```
<!DOCTYPE html>
<html>
<head>
  <title>{{ product.name }}</title>
</head>
<body>
  <h1>{{ product.name }}</h1>
  <p>Price: ${{ product.price }}</p>
  <p>{{ product.description }}</p>
</body>
</html>
```

In this example, the template displays the name, price, and description of a specific product, retrieved from the database in the view.

2. **Looping Through Data:**
   - Django templates allow you to iterate over lists, dictionaries, and other sequences using the {% for %} tag. This is essential for displaying multiple items, such as a list of products, blog posts, or users.

Example:

Python

```python
from django.shortcuts import render

def product_list_view(request):
products = Product.objects.all()
return render(request, 'product_list.html', {'products':
products})
```

HTML

```html
<!DOCTYPE html>
<html>
<head>
  <title>Products</title>
</head>
<body>
  <h1>Products</h1>
  <ul>
    {% for product in products %}
      <li>
                    <a href="/product/{{ product.id }}/">{{
product.name }}</a> - ${{ product.price }}
      </li>
    {% empty %}
      <li>No products found.</li>
    {% endfor %}
  </ul>
</body>
</html>
```

This template displays a list of products, with each product's
name and price. The {% for %} loop iterates over the

products list, and the {% empty %} block is displayed if the list is empty.

3. **Conditional Logic:**
   o You can use {% if %}, {% elif %}, {% else %}, and {% endif %} tags to display different content based on conditions. This is useful for things like displaying different messages to logged-in users and guests, or showing different content based on a user's permissions.

Example:

HTML

```
{% if user.is_authenticated %}
  <p>Welcome, {{ user.username }}!</p>
  <a href="/logout/">Logout</a>
{% else %}
        <p>Please <a href="/login/">login</a> or <a href="/register/">register</a>.</p>
{% endif %}
```

This template displays a personalized greeting to logged-in users and a login/registration link to guests.

4. **Form Handling:**
   o Django's form handling integrates seamlessly with templates. You can render forms, display

form errors, and process form submissions within your templates.

Example:

HTML

```
<form method="post">
    {% csrf_token %}
    {{ form.as_p }}
    <button type="submit">Submit</button>
    {% if form.errors %}
          <p style="color: red;">Please correct the errors
below.</p>
    {% endif %}
</form>
```

This template renders a form and displays any validation errors. The {% csrf_token %} tag is essential for security.

5. **Template Inheritance and Inclusion:**
   - As discussed previously, template inheritance ({% extends %}, {% block %}, {% endblock %}) and inclusion ({% include %}) allow you to structure your templates efficiently, avoiding code duplication and making your site easier to maintain.
6. **Static Files:**

- Static files (CSS, JavaScript, images) are essential for styling and adding interactivity to your dynamic HTML pages. You use the {% static %} tag to include these files correctly.

Example:

HTML

```
<!DOCTYPE html>
<html>
<head>
  <title>My Page</title>
  <link rel="stylesheet" href="{% static 'css/style.css' %}">
  <script src="{% static 'js/script.js' %}"></script>
</head>
<body>
  <img src="{% static 'images/logo.png' %}" alt="Logo">
  {# ... dynamic content ... #}
</body>
</html>
```

Real-World Examples
- **Social Media Platform:**
  - Dynamic HTML is used to display user profiles, posts, comments, notifications, and real-time updates.
  - Templates handle user authentication, post creation, and displaying personalized content.

- **E-commerce Website:**
  - Dynamic HTML is used to display product listings, product details, shopping carts, order summaries, and user account information.
  - Templates handle product searches, adding items to carts, processing orders, and managing user accounts.
- **News Website:**
  - Dynamic HTML is used to display articles, categories, search results, and user comments.
  - Templates handle content management, user interactions, and displaying related articles.

By effectively combining these techniques, you can build powerful and engaging web applications with Django, creating a rich and interactive experience for your users.

Chapter 8: Frontend Integration with JavaScript

Let's make our Django applications even more interactive! In this chapter, we'll explore how to use JavaScript to enhance the user experience. We'll learn how to include JavaScript in our templates, use AJAX to communicate with the backend, and optionally, how to integrate Django with frontend frameworks. Get ready to add some dynamic flair to your websites!

8.1 Integrating JavaScript with Django Templates

JavaScript is the language of the web browser. It allows you to manipulate web pages, respond to user actions, and perform various tasks on the client-side (in the user's browser). Django templates provide the canvas for integrating this dynamic behavior.

There are two primary ways to include JavaScript in your Django templates: inline JavaScript and external JavaScript files.

1. Inline JavaScript

Inline JavaScript involves writing your JavaScript code directly within `<script>` tags in your HTML template. This approach is suitable for small snippets of JavaScript code or when you need to directly access variables from your Django template.

Here's an example:

HTML

```
<!DOCTYPE html>
<html>
<head>
  <title>My Page</title>
</head>
<body>
  <button id="myButton">Click me</button>
  <p id="myParagraph"></p>

  <script>
    const button = document.getElementById('myButton');
    const paragraph = document.getElementById('myParagraph');
    button.addEventListener('click', function() {
    paragraph.textContent = 'Button clicked!';
    });
  </script>
</body>
</html>
```

In this code:

- We have a button and a paragraph.
- The <script> tags contain JavaScript code that:
  - Gets references to the button and paragraph using document.getElementById().
  - Adds an event listener to the button. When the button is clicked, the provided function is executed.

- The function changes the text content of the paragraph.

Accessing Template Variables in Inline JavaScript

A powerful feature of inline JavaScript is that you can directly access variables from your Django template's context. This allows you to make your JavaScript code dynamic.

Here's an example:

Python

```python
from django.shortcuts import render
def my_view(request):
    context = {
    'user_name': 'John Doe',
    'items': ['apple', 'banana', 'orange']
    }
    return render(request, 'my_template.html', context)
```

HTML

```html
<!DOCTYPE html>
<html>
<head>
  <title>My Page</title>
</head>
<body>
  <h1>Welcome, {{ user_name }}!</h1>
  <p>Here are your favorite fruits:</p>
```

```
<ul id="fruitList"></ul>
<script>
  const userName = "{{ user_name }}";
  const items = JSON.parse('{{ items|safe|escapejs }}');
  const fruitList = document.getElementById('fruitList');
  console.log("Welcome " + userName);
  items.forEach(item => {
  const li = document.createElement('li');
  li.textContent = item;
  fruitList.appendChild(li);
  });
</script>
</body>
</html>
```

In this example:

- We pass user_name and items from the view to the template.
- In the <script> tags:
  - const userName = "{{ user_name }}"; assigns the value of user_name to a JavaScript variable.
  - const items = JSON.parse('{{ items|safe|escapejs }}'); is important.
    - {{ items|safe|escapejs }}:
      - safe: Marks the output as safe, preventing Django from escaping HTML characters. This is necessary because items is a Python list, which could contain characters that need to be escaped for JavaScript.

- **escapejs:** Escapes characters that have special meaning in JavaScript. This is crucial for security to prevent potential issues if your data contains special characters.
  - **JSON.parse():** Parses the escaped JavaScript string back into a JavaScript array.
- The JavaScript code then uses these variables to display a personalized greeting and create a list of fruits.

2. External JavaScript Files

The more common and recommended approach for larger JavaScript codebases is to use external .js files. This promotes better code organization, reusability, and browser caching.

Here's how to use external JavaScript files:

1. **Create a static Directory:**
   - If you haven't already, make sure you have a static directory set up in your Django app (as explained in the chapter on static files).
   - Place your .js files in the static directory. For example:

```
myapp/
static/
 myapp/
js/
```

my_script.js

2. Link to the JavaScript File in Your Template:

- ○ Use the <script src="..."> tag to link to your .js file. Use the {% static %} template tag to generate the correct URL for the static file.

HTML

```
{% load static %}
<!DOCTYPE html>
<html>
<head>
  <title>My Page</title>
        <script    src="{%    static    'myapp/js/my_script.js'
%}"></script>
</head>
<body>
  {# ... your page content ... #}
</body>
</html>
```

Example: External JavaScript File (my_script.js)

JavaScript

```
console.log("Hello from my_script.js!");
const button = document.getElementById('myButton');
```

```
                const       paragraph      =
document.getElementById('myParagraph');
  if (button && paragraph) {
  button.addEventListener('click', function() {
    paragraph.textContent = 'Button clicked from external
file!';
  });
  }
```

Practical Considerations

- **Placement of** <script> **Tags:**
  - It's generally recommended to place <script> tags at the end of the <body> element, just before the closing </body> tag. This ensures that the HTML content is loaded and parsed before the JavaScript code tries to access it, preventing potential errors.
  - If you need to place <script> tags in the <head>, you can use the defer or async attributes to control when the script is executed.
- **Security:**
  - Be cautious when including external JavaScript files from third-party sources. Make sure you trust the source to avoid security vulnerabilities.
- **Performance:**
  - Minimize the number of external JavaScript files to reduce HTTP requests.
  - Use minification and bundling techniques to reduce the file size of your JavaScript code, improving page load times.

By understanding how to integrate JavaScript into your Django templates, you can create web pages that are not only visually appealing but also interactive and responsive to user actions.

8.2 Using AJAX to Fetch Data from the Backend

AJAX stands for Asynchronous JavaScript and XML. While the name includes "XML," modern AJAX typically uses JSON (JavaScript Object Notation) for data exchange, which is lighter and easier for JavaScript to handle.

The core idea behind AJAX is that you can use JavaScript to make HTTP requests to the server *in the background*, without interrupting the user's interaction with the page. When the server responds, JavaScript can then update parts of the page dynamically.

This leads to a much smoother user experience. Think about:
- **Live Search Suggestions:** As you type in a search bar, suggestions appear without the page reloading.
- **Dynamic Updates:** A news feed updating with new posts without you having to refresh.
- **Form Submissions:** Submitting a form and getting a confirmation message without leaving the page.

How AJAX Works

Here's a simplified breakdown of the process:

1. **JavaScript Initiates Request:** JavaScript code in the browser creates an HTTP request (GET, POST, etc.) to a specific URL on the server.
2. **Server Processes Request:** The server receives the request, processes it (e.g., retrieves data from a database), and prepares a response.
3. **Server Sends Response:** The server sends the response back to the browser. The response is often in JSON format.
4. **JavaScript Updates Page:** JavaScript code in the browser receives the response and updates the Document Object Model (DOM) – the structure of the web page – to reflect the new data.

Using the fetch **API**

The modern way to perform AJAX requests in JavaScript is to use the fetch API. It's built into most modern browsers and provides a clean and powerful interface.

Here's a basic example of using fetch to get data:

JavaScript

```
fetch('/my-api-endpoint/')  // The URL to request
  .then(response => {
    if (!response.ok) {
    throw new Error('Network response was not ok');
    }
      return response.json();  // Parse the response body as
JSON
  })
  .then(data => {
```

```
    // Do something with the data
    console.log(data);

document.getElementById('my-element').textContent    =
data.message;
    })
    .catch(error => {
    // Handle errors
        console.error('There was a problem fetching the
data:', error);
    });
  ```
```

Let's break this down:
- `fetch('/my-api-endpoint/')`: This initiates a GET request to the specified URL. `fetch` returns a Promise.
- `.then(response => { ... })`: This handles the response from the server.
- `if (!response.ok) { ... }`: This checks if the HTTP response status code indicates success (e.g., 200 OK). If not, it throws an error.
- `return response.json();`: This parses the response body as JSON and returns another Promise that resolves with the parsed data.
- `.then(data => { ... })`: This handles the parsed JSON data.
- `console.log(data);`: This logs the data to the console (useful for debugging).
- `document.getElementById('my-element').textContent = data.message;`: This updates the text content of an HTML element with the data from the response.
```

- `.catch(error => { ... })`: This handles any errors that occur during the fetch operation.

Sending Data with `fetch` (POST Requests)

To send data to the server (e.g., when submitting a form), you use the POST method and include the data in the request body.

```javascript
const data = { key1: 'value1', key2: 'value2' };
fetch('/my-api-endpoint/', {
  method: 'POST',
  headers: {
      'Content-Type': 'application/json',  // Tell the server we're sending JSON
      'X-CSRFToken': getCookie('csrftoken'), // Include CSRF token (Django security)
  },
      body: JSON.stringify(data),  // Convert data to JSON string
})
.then(response => {
  if (!response.ok) {
   throw new Error('Network response was not ok');
  }
  return response.json();
})
.then(data => {
  console.log('Success:', data);
  // Handle the server's response
})
```

```
.catch(error => {
  console.error('Error:', error);
});
```

Key points:

- method: 'POST': Specifies the HTTP method.
- headers: { ... }: Sets HTTP headers.
  - 'Content-Type': 'application/json': Tells the server that we're sending JSON data.
  - 'X-CSRFToken': getCookie('csrftoken'): This is crucial for Django security. Django requires a CSRF token to be included in POST requests to prevent Cross-Site Request Forgery attacks. You'll need a function like getCookie to retrieve the CSRF token from the browser's cookies (Django provides this in its documentation).
- body: JSON.stringify(data): Converts the JavaScript object data into a JSON string and includes it in the request body.

Django Views for AJAX

On the Django side, you'll need to create views that handle AJAX requests and **return appropriate responses. These views often return JSON data.**

Python

```
from django.http import JsonResponse
from django.views.decorators.csrf import csrf_exempt  # Be careful with this!
import json
```

```python
def my_api_view_get(request):
    if request.method == 'GET':
        data = {'message': 'Hello from the server!'}
        return JsonResponse(data)
    else:
        return JsonResponse({'error': 'Invalid request method'},
status=400)
    @csrf_exempt  # Only use this if you REALLY know what
you're doing
    def my_api_view_post(request):
    if request.method == 'POST':
        try:
            data = json.loads(request.body)
            # Process the data (e.g., save to database)
            print("Received data:", data)
                return JsonResponse({'message': 'Data received
successfully'})
        except json.JSONDecodeError:
                return JsonResponse({'error': 'Invalid JSON'},
status=400)
        else:
                return JsonResponse({'error': 'Invalid request
method'}, status=400)
```

Important notes:

- JsonResponse: This is a Django helper function that
  creates an HttpResponse with the Content-Type set to
  application/json.
- csrf_exempt: **Use this decorator with extreme caution!**
  It disables Django's CSRF protection for this view. Only
  use it if you have alternative security measures in place

(e.g., API keys). It's generally better to include the CSRF token in your AJAX requests as shown in the JavaScript example.

- json.loads(request.body): This parses the JSON data from the request body.

Real-World Examples

- **E-commerce Website:**
  - Adding items to a shopping cart without a page reload.
  - Displaying product suggestions as the user types in a search bar.
  - Updating the order total dynamically when the user changes the quantity of an item.
- **Social Media Platform:**
  - Loading new posts or comments without refreshing the page.
  - Submitting a like or comment without navigating away.
  - Displaying real-time notifications.

AJAX is a powerful tool for creating modern and interactive web applications. By understanding how to use fetch (or other AJAX libraries) and how to handle AJAX requests in your Django views, you can significantly enhance the user experience of your websites.

8.3 Working with Frontend Frameworks (e.g., integrating Vue.js or React with Django) (optional)

Frontend frameworks like Vue.js and React have become incredibly popular for building complex and dynamic user interfaces. They provide tools and libraries for managing UI components, handling user interactions, and creating Single Page Applications (SPAs).

When you integrate a frontend framework with Django, you typically use Django as a backend API. Django handles the server-side logic, database interactions, and authentication, while the frontend framework handles the presentation layer and user interactions in the browser.

This approach offers several advantages:

- **Separation of Concerns:** It clearly separates the backend logic (Django) from the frontend presentation (Vue.js/React), making your code more organized and maintainable.
- **Rich User Interfaces:** Frontend frameworks enable you to build highly interactive and responsive user interfaces.
- **Single Page Applications (SPAs):** You can create SPAs, where the user interacts with a single HTML page, and the frontend framework dynamically updates the content. This can provide a smoother and faster user experience.

- **Scalability:** This architecture can be very scalable, as you can optimize the backend and frontend independently.

Django as a Backend API

To integrate Django with a frontend framework, you'll need to create an API that the framework can consume. Django REST Framework (DRF) is the ideal tool for building RESTful APIs.

Here's a general workflow:

1. **Define Models and Serializers:** In your Django app, you define your data models and create DRF serializers to convert data between Python objects and JSON.
2. **Create API Views:** You create DRF views (often using ViewSets and Routers) to handle API requests and responses. These views use the serializers to interact with the models.
3. **Configure URLs:** You configure URL patterns to expose your API endpoints.
4. **Frontend Framework Consumes API:** Your Vue.js or React application makes HTTP requests to the Django API endpoints to retrieve and send data.

Example: Integrating Vue.js with Django

Let's illustrate the integration with a simplified example using Vue.js. We'll create a basic to-do list application.

Django (Backend)

1. **Define Model and Serializer:**

Python

```python
# myapp/models.py
from django.db import models
class Task(models.Model):
    title = models.CharField(max_length=200)
    completed = models.BooleanField(default=False)
    def __str__(self):
    return self.title


# myapp/serializers.py
from rest_framework import serializers
from .models import Task
class TaskSerializer(serializers.ModelSerializer):
    class Meta:
        model = Task
        fields = ('id', 'title', 'completed')
```

2. **Create API ViewSet:**

Python

```python
# myapp/views.py
from rest_framework import viewsets
from .models import Task
from .serializers import TaskSerializer
class TaskViewSet(viewsets.ModelViewSet):
    queryset = Task.objects.all()
    serializer_class = TaskSerializer
```

3. **Configure URLs:**

```python
# myproject/urls.py
from django.urls import path, include
from rest_framework import routers
from myapp import views
router = routers.DefaultRouter()
router.register(r'tasks', views.TaskViewSet)
urlpatterns = [
    path('api/', include(router.urls)),
]
```

Vue.js (Frontend)

1. **Set up Vue.js Project:**

   You'll need Node.js and npm (Node Package Manager) installed. You can create a Vue.js project using the Vue CLI:

```bash
npm install -g @vue/cli
vue create todo-frontend
cd todo-frontend
npm run serve
```

2. Vue.js Component to Fetch and Display Tasks:

JavaScript

```
// src/components/TaskList.vue
<template>
 <div>
  <h1>Tasks</h1>
  <ul>
  <li v-for="task in tasks" :key="task.id">
     {{ task.title }} - {{ task.completed ? 'Completed' :
'Pending' }}
  </li>
  </ul>
 </div>
</template>
<script>
import axios from 'axios';  // You'll need to install axios:
npm install axios
export default {
 data() {
  return {
   tasks: []
  };
 },
 mounted() {
  this.fetchTasks();
 },
 methods: {
```

```
  async fetchTasks() {
    try {
      const response = await axios.get('/api/tasks/'); // Fetch
from Django API
      this.tasks = response.data;
    } catch (error) {
    console.error('Error fetching tasks:', error);
    }
    }
  }
};
</script>
```

- ○ We use axios to make HTTP requests to the Django API.
- ○ data(): Defines the component's data (an empty array for tasks initially).
- ○ mounted(): This lifecycle hook is called when the component is mounted to the DOM. We call fetchTasks() here.
- ○ fetchTasks(): This method uses axios.get() to fetch tasks from the Django API (/api/tasks/).
- ○ The v-for directive iterates over the tasks array and displays each task.

3. **Include the Component in** App.vue:

Code snippet

```
<template>
  <div id="app">
```

```
<TaskList />
</div>
</template>
<script>
import TaskList from './components/TaskList.vue';
export default {
 components: {
  TaskList
 }
}
</script>
```

This simplified example demonstrates the basic structure:

- Django provides the API endpoints.
- Vue.js fetches data from those endpoints and displays it.

Important Considerations

- **CORS (Cross-Origin Resource Sharing):** If your Django and Vue.js applications are served from different origins (domains or ports), you'll need to configure CORS in your Django settings to allow requests from the Vue.js application. You can use the django-cors-headers package.
- **Authentication:** You'll need to implement authentication to secure your API. DRF provides various authentication methods.
- **State Management:** For larger applications, consider using a state management library like Vuex (for Vue.js) to manage the application's state.

- **Build Process:** You'll likely need a build process (e.g., using Webpack) to bundle and optimize your frontend assets for production.

Integrating frontend frameworks with Django opens up a world of possibilities for building modern and interactive web applications. While the initial setup might seem a bit more complex, the benefits in terms of code organization, maintainability, and user experience are significant.

8.4 Using Web Sockets with Django Channels

WebSockets provide a way to establish a persistent, two-way communication channel between a user's browser and a server. This is in contrast to the traditional HTTP request-response cycle, where the browser sends a request, and the server sends a response, and then the connection is closed.

WebSockets allow the server to push updates to the client without the client having to repeatedly request them. This is essential for applications like:

- **Chat Applications:** Sending and receiving messages in real-time.
- **Real-time Notifications:** Displaying instant updates to users.
- **Live Dashboards:** Showing continuously updated data.
- **Multiplayer Games:** Synchronizing game state between players.

Django Channels is a project that extends Django to handle WebSockets and other asynchronous protocols. It allows you to write Django views that can handle both HTTP requests and WebSocket connections.

Understanding the Challenges

Django is traditionally synchronous, meaning it processes one request at a time. WebSockets, on the other hand, are inherently asynchronous. They need to handle multiple connections concurrently and process messages in a non-blocking way.

Channels addresses this by providing an asynchronous layer on top of Django, allowing you to handle WebSockets efficiently.

Key Components of Django Channels

- **Channels:** The core of Channels. It's a routing system that directs incoming messages (both HTTP and WebSocket) to the appropriate consumers.
- **Consumers:** Asynchronous views that handle WebSocket connections. They define how to handle events like connecting, receiving messages, and disconnecting.
- **Channel Layers:** A communication system that allows different parts of your application (e.g., different consumers) to communicate with each other. This is crucial for scaling your application.
- **ASGI (Asynchronous Server Gateway Interface):** A standard for asynchronous Python web servers.

Channels requires an ASGI server (like Daphne) instead of a WSGI server (like Gunicorn).

Setting Up Django Channels

Here's a general outline of how to set up Django Channels:

1. **Install Channels:**

Bash

```
pip install channels
```

2. **Install an ASGI Server:**

Daphne is a popular ASGI server.

Bash

```
pip install daphne
```

3. **Add Channels to** INSTALLED_APPS:

Python

```
INSTALLED_APPS = [
    #  ...
    'channels',
```

```
#  ...
]
```

4. **Configure** ASGI_APPLICATION **in** settings.py:

Python

```
ASGI_APPLICATION   =   'myproject.asgi.application'      #
Replace 'myproject'
```

5. **Create** asgi.py:

This file tells Django which ASGI application to use.

Python

```
#  myproject/asgi.py
import os
from    channels.routing    import    ProtocolTypeRouter,
URLRouter
from django.core.asgi import get_asgi_application
from django.urls import path
os.environ.setdefault('DJANGO_SETTINGS_MODULE',
'myproject.settings')
application = ProtocolTypeRouter({
   'http': get_asgi_application(),
   'websocket': URLRouter([
     path('ws/chat/', consumers.ChatConsumer.as_asgi()),  #
Replace 'ws/chat/'
```

```
]),
})
```

- ProtocolTypeRouter: Routes connections based on the protocol (HTTP or WebSocket).
- get_asgi_application(): Handles HTTP requests.
- URLRouter: Routes WebSocket connections based on the URL path.
- consumers.ChatConsumer.as_asgi(): Specifies the consumer that will handle WebSocket connections to the /ws/chat/ path.

6. **Define Consumers:**

Consumers are asynchronous classes that handle WebSocket connections.

Python

```python
# myapp/consumers.py
import json
from channels.generic.websocket import AsyncWebsocketConsumer
class ChatConsumer(AsyncWebsocketConsumer):
    async def connect(self):
        await self.accept()
    async def disconnect(self, close_code):
        pass
    async def receive(self, text_data):
        text_data_json = json.loads(text_data)
        message = text_data_json['message']
```

```
await self.send(text_data=json.dumps({
  'message': message
}))
```

- AsyncWebsocketConsumer: A base class for handling WebSocket connections asynchronously.
- connect(): Called when a client first connects. self.accept() accepts the connection.
- disconnect(): Called when a client disconnects.
- receive(): Called when the server receives a message from the client.
  - json.loads(): Parses the incoming JSON data.
  - self.send(): Sends data back to the client. json.dumps() converts the data to a JSON string.

7. **Run the ASGI Server:**

Bash

```
daphne myproject.asgi:application  # Replace 'myproject'
```

Practical Example: A Simple Echo Server

The consumer example above implements a simple "echo" server. It receives a message from the client and sends the same message back.

Frontend (JavaScript)

JavaScript

```javascript
    const chatSocket = new WebSocket('ws://' +
window.location.host + '/ws/chat/');
  chatSocket.onmessage = function(e) {
    const data = JSON.parse(e.data);
    console.log('Message received:', data.message);
      document.getElementById('chat-log').textContent +=
data.message + '\n';
  };
  chatSocket.onopen = function(e) {
    console.log('Connection established');
  };
  chatSocket.onclose = function(e) {
    console.error('Chat socket closed unexpectedly');
  };

document.getElementById('chat-message-input').onkeyup
= function(e) {
    if (e.key === 'Enter') { // Send message on Enter key
                              const message =
document.getElementById('chat-message-input').value;
      chatSocket.send(JSON.stringify({ 'message': message
}));

document.getElementById('chat-message-input').value = '';
    }
  };
```

- new WebSocket(): Creates a WebSocket connection to
  the server.

- **chatSocket.onmessage**: Handles incoming messages from the server.
- **chatSocket.onopen**: Handles the connection opening.
- **chatSocket.onclose**: Handles the connection closing.
- **chatSocket.send()**: Sends a message to the server.

Important Considerations

- **Channel Layers**: For more complex applications, you'll need to configure a channel layer (e.g., Redis, in-memory) to handle communication between different consumers.
- **Asynchronous Programming**: Channels requires you to write asynchronous code, which can be different from traditional Django programming.
- **Deployment**: Deploying Channels applications requires an ASGI server and careful consideration of scaling and load balancing.

Django Channels provides a powerful way to add real-time functionality to your Django projects. While it introduces some complexity, it enables you to build modern and interactive web applications that can communicate with users in real time.

Chapter 9: Forms and User Interfaces

Let's make our Django applications interactive and secure! In this chapter, we're going to explore how to work with forms, which are the primary way users interact with your application. We'll learn how to create and customize forms, handle user authentication, and build attractive interfaces with HTML and CSS. Get ready to create user-friendly and secure web experiences!

9.1 Building Complex Forms with Django Forms

Django's Form class is much more than just a way to generate HTML input fields. It's a comprehensive system for defining form fields, handling user input, validating data, and cleaning data for use in your application.

Understanding Django Forms

A Django form is a Python class that defines the fields of your form, their data types, how they should be rendered, and the rules for validating the user's input. This object-oriented approach provides a structured and maintainable way to work with forms.

Here's a breakdown of the key aspects of Django forms:

- **Form Fields:** These define the individual input elements of your form, such as text boxes, dropdown lists, checkboxes, etc. Django provides a wide variety of built-in form fields.

- **Form Widgets:** These control how the form fields are rendered in HTML. For example, a CharField can be rendered as a simple <input type="text"> or a <textarea>.
- **Validation:** Django forms automatically validate user input based on the field types and any custom validation rules you define. This ensures that the data you receive from the user is in the correct format and meets your application's requirements.
- **Data Cleaning:** Django forms "clean" the submitted data, converting it to the appropriate Python types and handling potential security issues.

Creating Django Forms

You define forms as Python classes that inherit from Django's Form class.

Here's an example of a form for submitting a support ticket:

Python

```python
from django import forms
class SupportTicketForm(forms.Form):
    subject = forms.CharField(
        label="Subject",
        max_length=100,
        help_text="Enter a brief subject for your ticket."
    )
    description = forms.CharField(
        label="Description",
```

```python
        widget=forms.Textarea,
        help_text="Provide a detailed description of the issue."
    )
    priority = forms.ChoiceField(
        label="Priority",
        choices=[
            ('low', 'Low'),
            ('medium', 'Medium'),
            ('high', 'High'),
        ],
        initial='medium',
        help_text="Select the priority of your ticket."
    )
    attachment = forms.FileField(
        label="Attachment (optional)",
        required=False,
        help_text="Attach any relevant files (max. 1MB)."
    )
    cc_email = forms.BooleanField(
        label="Send a copy to my email",
        required=False,
        initial=True,
            help_text="Check this box to receive a copy of this
ticket."
    )
    def clean_description(self):
        description = self.cleaned_data['description']
        if len(description) < 10:
        raise forms.ValidationError("Description must be at least
10 characters long.")
        return description
    def clean_attachment(self):
```

```
attachment = self.cleaned_data.get('attachment')
if attachment:
if attachment.size > 1024 * 1024:  # 1MB
    raise forms.ValidationError("Attachment size exceeds
1MB.")
return attachment
```

Let's break down this example:

- **forms.CharField**: This field is used for single-line text input.
  - **label**: A user-friendly label for the field.
  - **max_length**: The maximum allowed length of the input.
  - **help_text**: A helpful description displayed alongside the field.
- **forms.CharField(widget=forms.Textarea)**: This renders a multi-line text input area.
- **forms.ChoiceField**: This field presents a dropdown list of choices.
  - **choices**: A list of tuples, where each tuple contains the value and the display name of a choice.
  - **initial**: The default selected value.
- **forms.FileField**: This field allows users to upload files.
  - **required=False**: Makes the field optional.
- **forms.BooleanField**: This field renders a checkbox.
  - **initial=True**: Sets the checkbox to be checked by default.

Custom Validation

Django provides built-in validation for many field types (e.g., EmailField validates email addresses). However, you can also add custom validation logic:

- **Field-Specific Validation** (clean_<field_name>):
  - You can define a method named clean_<field_name> in your form class to perform custom validation for a specific field.
  - This method receives the cleaned value of the field as input and should either return the cleaned value or raise a forms.ValidationError if the value is invalid.
  - In the example, clean_description and clean_attachment provide custom validation for the description and attachment fields.
- **Form-Wide Validation** (clean):
  - You can define a method named clean in your form class to perform validation that involves multiple fields.
  - This method should return the cleaned data or raise a forms.ValidationError if the form data is invalid.

Practical Considerations

- **Help Text:** Always provide clear and concise help_text to guide users in filling out the form.
- **Error Handling:** Django forms automatically handle the display of validation errors. You can customize the error messages if needed.

- **Security:** Be aware of security best practices when handling form data, such as escaping user input to prevent XSS attacks.

Real-World Examples

- **User Registration Forms:** These forms often involve complex validation rules for passwords, email addresses, and usernames.
- **E-commerce Checkout Forms:** These forms may need to handle various payment options, shipping addresses, and order summaries.
- **Data Entry Forms:** These forms can be used to collect structured data from users, such as survey responses or product information.

By mastering Django forms, you can create powerful and user-friendly interfaces for collecting and processing user input in your web applications.

9.2 Customizing Form Rendering

Django gives you several ways to control how your forms are displayed in HTML. You can choose the level of customization that best suits your needs, from simple tweaks to complete control over the HTML structure.

Understanding Form Rendering

By default, Django renders forms using the as_p(), as_ul(), and as_table() methods. These methods provide a quick way to display the form, but they offer limited control over the HTML.

Here's a recap:

- form.as_p(): Renders the form fields wrapped in <p> tags.
- form.as_ul(): Renders the form fields as a list (using <ul> and <li> tags).
- form.as_table(): Renders the form fields within a table (using <table>, <tr>, and <td> tags).

For more complex or specific styling, you'll need to customize the rendering.

1. Manual Rendering of Form Fields

Manual rendering gives you the most granular control over the HTML output. You render each form field individually, allowing you to specify the exact HTML elements, CSS classes, and attributes you want to use.

Here's how it works:

- **Form Attributes:**
  - form.label_tag(): Renders the <label> tag for the field.
  - form.field: Renders the input field itself.
  - form.errors: Provides any validation errors for the field.
- **Template Structure:**
  - You'll need to structure the HTML for your form, including the <form> tag, and then use the form

field attributes to insert the appropriate elements.

Here's an example:

HTML

```
<form method="post">
  {% csrf_token %}
  <div class="form-group">
    {{ form.subject.label_tag }}
    {{ form.subject }}
    {% if form.subject.errors %}
    <div class="alert alert-danger">
    {{ form.subject.errors }}
    </div>
    {% endif %}
              <small class="form-text text-muted">{{ form.subject.help_text }}</small>
  </div>
  <div class="form-group">
    {{ form.description.label_tag }}
    {{ form.description }}
    {% if form.description.errors %}
    <div class="alert alert-danger">
    {{ form.description.errors }}
    </div>
    {% endif %}
              <small class="form-text text-muted">{{ form.description.help_text }}</small>
  </div>
```

```
<div class="form-group">
  {{ form.priority.label_tag }}
  {{ form.priority }}
  {% if form.priority.errors %}
  <div class="alert alert-danger">
  {{ form.priority.errors }}
  </div>
  {% endif %}
              <small  class="form-text  text-muted">{{
form.priority.help_text }}</small>
  </div>
                  <button   type="submit"   class="btn
btn-primary">Submit</button>
  </form>
```

In this example:

- We manually render the subject, description, and priority fields.
- We use CSS classes (form-group, alert, btn) to style the form elements (you'd need to define these in your CSS file).
- We display validation errors using form.field.errors.
- We display help text using form.field.help_text.
- form.subject.label_tag() renders the <label> tag for the subject field, including any necessary for attribute to associate it with the input.
- form.subject renders the input field itself (e.g., <input type="text">).

2. Form Templates

For more complex customization or when you want to reuse form rendering logic, you can create custom template tags or template snippets.

- **Template Snippets:**
  - You can create a small template file (e.g., form_field.html) that renders a single form field in a consistent way.
  - You can then use the {% include %} tag to include this template in your main form template.

Here's an example:

form_field.html:

HTML

```
<div class="form-group">
   {{ field.label_tag }}
   {{ field }}
   {% if field.errors %}
     <div class="alert alert-danger">
     { field.errors }}
     </div>
   {% endif %}
   {% if field.help_text %}
               <small class="form-text text-muted">{{
field.help_text }}</small>
   {% endif %}
</div>
```

Main form template:

HTML

```
<form method="post">
    {% csrf_token %}
    {% include 'form_field.html' with field=form.subject %}
        {% include 'form_field.html' with
field=form.description %}
    {% include 'form_field.html' with field=form.priority
%}
        <button type="submit" class="btn
btn-primary">Submit</button>
</form>
```

{% include 'form_field.html' with field=form.subject %}:
This includes the form_field.html template and passes the
form.subject field to it.

- **Custom Template Tags:**
    - ○ For more advanced customization, you can
      create custom template tags that render form
      fields or entire forms.
    - ○ This is useful if you need to perform complex
      logic or generate highly customized HTML.

Practical Considerations

- **Consistency:** Aim for consistency in your form
  rendering. Use the same styling and layout for all forms
  on your website.

- **Accessibility:** Ensure that your forms are accessible to users with disabilities. Use proper HTML semantics, provide clear labels, and handle errors effectively.
- **CSS Frameworks:** Consider using a CSS framework like Bootstrap or Tailwind CSS to speed up form styling and create responsive layouts.

Real-World Examples

- **E-commerce Website:**
  - You might customize the rendering of the checkout form to match your website's branding and provide a clear and user-friendly checkout process.
- **Social Media Platform:**
  - You might customize the rendering of the user registration form to provide a visually appealing and informative registration experience.
- **Dashboard Application:**
  - You might customize the rendering of data filtering forms to provide a clean and efficient way for users to filter and analyze data.

By mastering form rendering in Django, you can create forms that are not only functional but also visually appealing and user-friendly, enhancing the overall user experience of your web application.

9.3 Implementing User Authentication and Authorization

When building a web application, you'll often need to manage user accounts and control access to different parts of your site.[1] This involves two key processes:

- **Authentication:** Verifying the identity of a user.[2]
- **Authorization:** Determining what an authenticated user is permitted to do.[3]

Django provides a robust built-in authentication and authorization system that simplifies these tasks.[4]

Understanding User Authentication

Authentication is the process of confirming that a user is who they claim to be.[5] The most common way to do this on the web is with usernames and passwords.

Here's how Django's authentication system works in a nutshell:

1. **User Model:** Django has a built-in User model (django.contrib.auth.models.User) that stores user information like username, password, email, etc. You can also create custom user models if you have specific requirements.[6]
2. **Authentication Backends:** Django uses authentication backends to verify user credentials.[7] The default backend checks the username and password against the User model in your database.

3. **Authentication Forms:** Django provides forms (AuthenticationForm) to handle the login process.
4. **Login and Logout:** Django provides functions (login(), logout()) to log users in and out.
5. **Session Management:** Django uses sessions to maintain the logged-in state of a user across multiple requests.[8]

Practical Implementation: User Registration, Login, and Logout

Let's walk through a common authentication workflow: user registration, login, and logout.

1. User Registration

While you *can* use Django's UserCreationForm for registration, it's often a good idea to create a custom form to have more control over the registration process.

Python

```
from django import forms
from django.contrib.auth.forms import UserCreationForm
from django.contrib.auth.models import User
class CustomUserCreationForm(UserCreationForm):
    email = forms.EmailField(label="Email")
    class Meta:
        model = User
        fields = ("username", "email")
#  views.py
from django.shortcuts import render, redirect
from .forms import CustomUserCreationForm
```

```python
from django.contrib import messages

def register_view(request):
    if request.method == "POST":
        form = CustomUserCreationForm(request.POST)
        if form.is_valid():
        user = form.save()
            messages.success(request, "Registration successful. You can now log in.")
        return redirect("login")  # Redirect to the login page
        else:
            return render(request, "registration/register.html", {"form": form})
    else:
        form = CustomUserCreationForm()
            return render(request, "registration/register.html", {"form": form})
```

We create a CustomUserCreationForm that inherits from Django's UserCreationForm to get the basic username and password fields. We then add an email field.

- In the register_view, we handle both GET and POST requests:
    - **GET:** Display the registration form.
    - **POST:** Process the submitted form data. If the form is valid, we create a new user, display a success message, and redirect to the login page.

2. User Login

Django's AuthenticationForm is used to handle the login process.

Python

```
# views.py
from django.shortcuts import render, redirect
from django.contrib.auth import authenticate, login
from django.contrib.auth.forms import AuthenticationForm
from django.contrib import messages


def login_view(request):
    if request.method == "POST":
        form = AuthenticationForm(request, data=request.POST)
        if form.is_valid():
            username = form.cleaned_data.get("username")
            password = form.cleaned_data.get("password")
            user = authenticate(username=username, password=password)
            if user is not None:
                login(request, user)
                messages.success(request, f"You are now logged in as {username}.")
                return redirect("home")  # Redirect to the home page
            else:
                messages.error(request, "Invalid username or password.")
        else:
```

```
        messages.error(request, "Invalid username or
password.")
        return render(request, "registration/login.html",
{"form": form})
    else:
        form = AuthenticationForm(request)
        return render(request, "registration/login.html",
{"form": form})
```

- We use Django's built-in AuthenticationForm.
- In the login_view:
    - **GET:** Display the login form.
    - **POST:** Process the submitted form data:
        - We validate the form.
        - We use authenticate() to check the username and password against the database.
        - If authenticate() returns a User object, we use login() to log the user in.
        - We redirect to the home page (or another appropriate page).
        - We handle invalid login attempts and display error messages.[9]

3. User Logout

Django provides a simple logout() function to log users out.

Python

```
# views.py
```

```
from django.contrib.auth import logout
from django.shortcuts import redirect
from django.contrib import messages
def logout_view(request):
    logout(request)
    messages.info(request, "You have been logged out.")
    return redirect("home")  # Redirect to the home page
```

- We simply call logout() and redirect the user.

Understanding User Authorization

Authorization is the process of determining what an authenticated user is allowed to do.[10] Django provides a powerful permissions system to manage this.[11]

Here are the key concepts:

- **Permissions:** Django has a built-in permission system that allows you to define specific actions that users can perform (e.g., "add_post," "change_post," "delete_post").[12]
- **Groups:** You can organize users into groups and assign permissions to those groups.[13] This makes it easier to manage permissions for large numbers of users.
- has_perm(): The user.has_perm() method checks if a user has a specific permission.
- **Decorators:** Django provides decorators (@login_required, @permission_required) to restrict access to views based on authentication and permissions.

Practical Implementation: Restricting Access to Views

Python

```python
# views.py
from django.contrib.auth.decorators import login_required, permission_required
from django.shortcuts import render
@login_required
def my_protected_view(request):
    return render(request, "my_protected_template.html")
@permission_required("myapp.add_post", raise_exception=True)
def my_permission_required_view(request):
    return render(request, "my_permission_required_template.html")
```

- @login_required: This decorator ensures that only authenticated users can access the my_protected_view. If an unauthenticated user tries to access it, they'll be redirected to the login page.
- @permission_required("myapp.add_post", raise_exception=True): This decorator ensures that only users with the "myapp.add_post" permission can access the my_permission_required_view.
  - "myapp.add_post": The permission is specified as "app_label.codename".
  - raise_exception=True: If the user doesn't have the permission, a PermissionDenied exception is raised (which Django will handle by displaying a "403 Forbidden" error).

Real-World Examples

- **E-commerce Website:**
  - Authentication: Users need to log in to place orders or view their order history.
  - Authorization: Only administrators can create or edit products.
- **Social Media Platform:**
  - Authentication: Users need to register and log in to create posts, follow other users, etc.[14]
  - Authorization: Users can only delete their own posts. Moderators can delete any post.
- **Content Management System (CMS):**
  - Authentication: Authors need to log in to write and edit articles.
  - Authorization: Editors can publish articles.

By understanding and implementing Django's authentication and authorization features, you can build secure and user-friendly web applications that protect your data and control access to your resources.

9.4 Creating User-Friendly Interfaces with HTML and CSS

When you build a web application, it's not just about functionality; it's also about how it looks and feels to the user. A well-designed interface can make your application more enjoyable to use, increase user engagement, and improve overall satisfaction.

Understanding HTML

HTML (Hypertext Markup Language) is the standard markup language for creating web pages. It provides the structure and content of[1] a web page. Think of it as the skeleton of your website.

Here are some key HTML concepts:

- **Tags:** HTML uses tags to define elements on a page. Tags are enclosed in angle brackets (<>). Most tags come in pairs: an opening tag (<p>) and a closing tag (</p>).
- **Elements:** An HTML element consists of an opening tag, content, and a closing tag. For example, <p>This is a paragraph.</p> is a paragraph element.
- **Attributes:** Tags can have attributes that provide additional information about the element. For example, <a href="https://www.example.com">Link</a> has the href attribute, which specifies the URL of the link.
- **Structure:** HTML elements are nested to create the structure of a web page. Common structural elements include:
  - <html>: The root element of an HTML page.
  - <head>: Contains metadata about the page, such as the title, links to CSS files, and scripts.
  - <body>: Contains the visible content of the page.
  - <header>: Represents the header of a section or page.
  - <footer>: Represents the footer of a section or page.
  - <nav>: Represents navigation elements.

- o <main>: Represents the main content of a document.
  - o <section>: Represents a thematic grouping of content.
  - o <article>: Represents a self-contained composition[2] (e.g., a blog post).
- **Content:** HTML provides elements for different types of content:
  - o <p>: Paragraph.
  - o <h1> to <h6>: Headings (different levels of importance).
  - o <a>: Link.
  - o <img>: Image.
  - o <ul>, <ol>, <li>: Unordered list, ordered list, list item.
  - o <table>, <tr>, <td>: Table, table row, table data cell.
  - o <form>, <input>, <button>: Form, input field, button.

Example HTML Structure

HTML

```
<!DOCTYPE html>
<html lang="en">
<head>
<meta charset="UTF-8">
<meta name="viewport" content="width=device-width, initial-scale=1.0">
<title>My Web Page</title>
```

```html
    <link rel="stylesheet" href="style.css">
  </head>
  <body>
    <header>
    <h1>Welcome to My Website</h1>
    <nav>
                                <a   href="/">Home</a>  |  <a
href="/about/">About</a>                |                <a
href="/contact/">Contact</a>
      </nav>
    </header>

    <main>
      <article>
      <h2>This is an Article</h2>
      <p>This is the content of the article.</p>
      <img src="my_image.jpg" alt="An image">
      </article>
      <section>
        <h3>Section Heading</h3>
        <ul>
          <li>Item 1</li>
          <li>Item 2</li>
          <li>Item 3</li>
        </ul>
      </section>
      <form action="/submit/" method="post">
      <label for="name">Name:</label>
      <input type="text" id="name" name="name">
      <button type="submit">Submit</button>
      </form>
    </main>
```

```
<footer>
<p>&copy; 2024 My Website</p>
</footer>
</body>
</html>
```

Understanding CSS

CSS (Cascading Style Sheets) is used to style the presentation of HTML elements. It controls how your web pages look, including colors, fonts, layout, and responsiveness. Think of it as the makeup for your website's skeleton.

Here are some key CSS concepts:

- **Selectors:** CSS uses selectors to target specific HTML elements that you want to style. Common selectors include:
  - element: Selects all elements of a given type (e.g., p selects all paragraph elements).
  - #id: Selects the element with the given ID (e.g., #header selects the element with id="header"). IDs should be unique within a page.
  - .class: Selects all elements with the given class (e.g., .button selects all elements with class="button"). Classes can be used multiple times on a page.
- **Properties:** CSS properties define the style of an element (e.g., color, font-size, background-color).
- **Values:** CSS properties are assigned values (e.g., color: blue;, font-size: 16px;).

- **Rulesets:** A CSS ruleset consists of a selector and a block of declarations (property-value pairs) enclosed in curly braces {}.

Example CSS Styles

CSS

```
body {
  font-family: sans-serif;
  margin: 0;
  padding: 0;
}
header {
  background-color: #f0f0f0;
  padding: 10px;
  text-align: center;
}
nav a {
  margin: 0 10px;
}

main {
  padding: 20px;
}
article {
  border-bottom: 1px solid #ccc;
  margin-bottom: 20px;
  padding-bottom: 20px;
}
.button {
  background-color: #4CAF50;
```

```
    color: white;
    padding: 10px 20px;
    border: none;
    cursor: pointer;
  }
```

Connecting HTML and CSS

You can apply CSS styles to your HTML in a few ways:

- **Inline Styles:** You can add styles directly to HTML elements using the style attribute (e.g., <p style="color: red;">). This is generally not recommended for large projects.
- **Internal Styles:** You can embed CSS within the <head> section of your HTML using the <style> tag.
- **External Styles:** The most common and recommended approach is to link to external CSS files using the <link> tag in the <head> section.

HTML

```
<head>
  <link rel="stylesheet" href="style.css">
</head>
```

Best Practices for User-Friendly Interfaces

Here are some key best practices for creating user-friendly interfaces with HTML and CSS:

- **Clear Structure:** Use semantic HTML elements to structure your content logically. This improves accessibility and SEO.
- **Consistent Design:** Use consistent colors, fonts, and spacing to create a cohesive visual experience.
- **Responsive Design:** Ensure that your interface adapts to different screen sizes and devices. Use CSS media queries to achieve this.
- **Accessibility:** Make your interface accessible to users with disabilities. Use proper ARIA attributes, provide alternative text for images, and ensure sufficient color contrast.
- **Performance:** Optimize your HTML and CSS to minimize page load times. Use minification, compression, and caching techniques.
- **Usability:** Design your interface to be intuitive and easy to use. Follow common UI patterns and provide clear feedback to user actions.

Real-World Examples

- **E-commerce Website:**
  - HTML: Structures product listings, product details pages, shopping cart, and checkout process.
  - CSS: Styles the layout, colors, fonts, and interactive elements of the website.
- **Social Media Platform:**
  - HTML: Structures user profiles, news feeds, messaging interfaces, and notification systems.

- CSS: Styles the visual appearance of posts, comments, user interactions, and platform branding.

By mastering HTML and CSS and following best practices, you can create user-friendly and visually appealing web interfaces that enhance the user experience and contribute to the success of your web applications.

Chapter 10: Testing Your Django Application

Let's learn how to make sure our code works correctly! In this chapter, we'll explore testing in Django. We'll cover writing unit tests and integration tests, using Django's testing tools, and even briefly discuss Test-Driven Development (TDD). Get ready to build more reliable and maintainable applications!

10.1 Writing Unit Tests and Integration Tests

Testing helps you ensure that your code behaves as expected, catches bugs early, and makes your code more maintainable. In the context of Django, we commonly talk about two main categories of tests: unit tests and integration tests.

Unit Tests

Unit tests focus on testing individual units of code in isolation. A "unit" can be a function, a method, or a class. The goal of a unit test is to verify that a specific piece of code works correctly, independent of other parts of the system.

Here's what's important to understand about unit tests:

- **Isolation:** Unit tests should be isolated. They should not rely on external dependencies like databases, file systems, or network connections. If your unit of code interacts with a database, you should use mocking or patching techniques to simulate the database interaction without actually hitting the database.

- **Speed:** Unit tests should be fast to run. Because you'll often run them frequently during development, slow unit tests can significantly slow down your workflow.
- **Focus:** Each unit test should focus on testing one specific aspect of the unit's behavior. This makes it easier to pinpoint the source of a bug when a test fails.

Example: Unit Testing a Simple Function

Let's say you have a simple function that calculates the total price of an order:

Python

```python
def calculate_total(price, quantity, discount=0):
    """Calculates the total price of an order."""
    total = price * quantity * (1 - discount)
    return round(total, 2)
```

Here's how you might write unit tests for this function:

Python

```python
import unittest
class TestCalculateTotal(unittest.TestCase):
    def test_calculate_total_without_discount(self):
    self.assertEqual(calculate_total(10, 2), 20)
    def test_calculate_total_with_discount(self):
    self.assertEqual(calculate_total(10, 2, 0.1), 18)
    def test_calculate_total_with_zero_quantity(self):
    self.assertEqual(calculate_total(10, 0), 0)
    def test_calculate_total_with_large_numbers(self):
        self.assertEqual(calculate_total(1000, 100), 100000)
```

```
if __name__ == '__main__':
    unittest.main()
```

- We use Python's built-in unittest framework.
- We create a test class TestCalculateTotal that inherits from unittest.TestCase.
- Each test method name starts with test_.
- We use self.assertEqual() to assert that the actual result of the function call matches the expected result.
- Each test method focuses on a specific scenario (e.g., with or without discount, zero quantity, large numbers).
- if __name__ == '__main__': unittest.main() runs the tests if the script is executed directly.

Integration Tests

Integration tests, on the other hand, focus on testing how different parts of your application work *together*. They verify that the interactions between components are correct.

Here's what's important to understand about integration tests:

- **Component Interaction:** Integration tests check the flow of data and control between different parts of your system. This might involve testing how a view interacts with a model, how different modules in your application communicate, or how your application interacts with external services.
- **Larger Scope:** Integration tests typically cover a larger scope than unit tests. They test a feature or a user workflow rather than a single function.

- **Dependencies:** Integration tests may involve real dependencies, such as databases or external APIs. However, it's often a good practice to use test databases or mock external services to ensure test reliability and speed.

Example: Integration Testing a Django View

Let's say you have a Django view that creates a new product:

Python

```
from django.shortcuts import render, redirect
from django.http import HttpResponse
from .models import Product
from .forms import ProductForm
def create_product(request):
  if request.method == 'POST':
    form = ProductForm(request.POST)
    if form.is_valid():
    form.save()
    return redirect('product_list')
    else:
      return render(request, 'create_product.html', {'form':
form})
    else:
      form = ProductForm()
      return render(request, 'create_product.html', {'form':
form})
```

Here's an example of an integration test for this view (using Django's testing tools):

Python

```python
from django.test import Client, TestCase
from django.urls import reverse
from .models import Product
class TestCreateProductView(TestCase):
    def setUp(self):
    self.client = Client()
        self.create_product_url = reverse('create_product')  # Assuming you have a URL named 'create_product'
    def test_create_product_success(self):
    response = self.client.post(self.create_product_url, {'name': 'Test Product', 'price': 10.00})
        self.assertEqual(response.status_code, 302)  # Check for redirect
        self.assertEqual(Product.objects.count(), 1)  # Check if product was created
    def test_create_product_invalid_data(self):
        response = self.client.post(self.create_product_url, {'name': '', 'price': 10.00})
    self.assertEqual(response.status_code, 200)  # Check for success (form re-rendered)
        self.assertEqual(Product.objects.count(), 0)  # Check if product was NOT created
```

- We use Django's TestCase, which provides a test database.
- self.client simulates a user's browser.
- reverse('create_product') gets the URL for the view by its name.
- We test both successful and unsuccessful form submissions.

- We check the HTTP status code of the response and the state of the database.

10.2 Using Django's Testing Tools

Django's testing framework is based on Python's unittest module, but it adds some Django-specific features and utilities that are tailored for testing web applications.

Key Components

Here are the main components of Django's testing framework:

- **Test Cases:** Django provides classes that you can inherit from to create your test suites. These classes provide helpful methods for setting up and tearing down your test environment, as well as assertion methods for verifying your code's behavior.
- **Assertions:** Assertions are methods that you use to check if a condition is true or false. They're the core of your tests, allowing you to verify that your code is producing the expected results.
- **Test Runner:** Django's test runner is a command-line tool that discovers and executes your tests. It provides options for running specific tests, controlling the output, and more.

1. Test Cases

Django provides several test case classes that are useful for different types of testing:

- `TestCase`: This is the most commonly used test case class. It automatically handles creating and destroying a test database for each test method. This ensures that your tests are isolated and don't affect your development database.
- `SimpleTestCase`: This class is similar to `TestCase` but doesn't create a test database. It's useful for testing code that doesn't interact with the database, such as utility functions or template filters. This makes these tests run faster.
- `TransactionTestCase`: This class is similar to `TestCase` but wraps each test method in a database transaction. This can be useful for testing database-related code that needs to be rolled back after the test.

Example: Using TestCase

Let's create a simple Django app and write some tests for it.

myapp/models.py:

Python

```python
from django.db import models
class Item(models.Model):
    name = models.CharField(max_length=200)
    description = models.TextField()
    price = models.DecimalField(max_digits=10, decimal_places=2)
```

```python
def __str__(self):
    return self.name
```

myapp/views.py:

Python

```python
from django.shortcuts import render
from django.http import HttpResponse
from .models import Item
def item_list(request):
    items = Item.objects.all()
    return render(request, 'myapp/item_list.html', {'items': items})
def item_detail(request, item_id):
    try:
        item = Item.objects.get(pk=item_id)
        return render(request, 'myapp/item_detail.html', {'item': item})
    except Item.DoesNotExist:
        return HttpResponse("Item not found", status=404)
```

myapp/tests.py:

Python

```python
from django.test import TestCase, Client
from django.urls import reverse
from .models import Item
class ItemViewsTestCase(TestCase):
    def setUp(self):
        #  Set up data that will be used in multiple tests
```

```python
        self.item1 = Item.objects.create(name="Test Item 1",
description="Description 1", price=10.00)
        self.item2 = Item.objects.create(name="Test Item 2",
description="Description 2", price=20.00)
    self.client = Client()  #  Simulates a user's browser
    def test_item_list_view(self):
        #  Test the item_list view
        url = reverse('item_list')  #  Get the URL for the view
by its name
        response = self.client.get(url)
        self.assertEqual(response.status_code, 200)  #  Check
if the response is OK
                        self.assertTemplateUsed(response,
'myapp/item_list.html')  #  Check if the correct template is
used
        self.assertEqual(len(response.context['items']), 2)  #
Check if all items are passed to the template
    def test_item_detail_view_existing_item(self):
        #  Test the item_detail view for an existing item
        url = reverse('item_detail', args=[self.item1.id])
        response = self.client.get(url)
        self.assertEqual(response.status_code, 200)
                        self.assertTemplateUsed(response,
'myapp/item_detail.html')
        self.assertEqual(response.context['item'], self.item1)
#  Check if the correct item is passed to the template
    def test_item_detail_view_nonexistent_item(self):
        #  Test the item_detail view for a non-existent item
        url = reverse('item_detail', args=[999])  #  An ID that
doesn't exist
        response = self.client.get(url)
```

self.assertEqual(response.status_code, 404) # Check if the response is 404 (Not Found)

We create a test class `ItemViewsTestCase` that inherits from `TestCase`.

- `setUp()`: This method is called before each test method in the class. It's used to set up any data or resources that will be needed by the tests. In this case, we create two `Item` objects and a `Client` instance.
- `self.client`: This is a Django `Client` object that simulates a user's browser. You can use it to make requests to your views.
- `reverse('item_list')`: This function from `django.urls` is used to get the URL for the view with the name "item_list." This is a best practice because it makes your tests more robust to changes in your URL configuration.
- `self.assertEqual()`: This is an assertion method that checks if two values are equal.
- `self.assertTemplateUsed()`: This assertion method checks if a specific template was used to render the response.
- `response.context`: This attribute of the `response` object provides access to the context data that was passed to the template.

2. Assertions

Django's test framework provides a rich set of assertion methods that you can use to verify different aspects of your code's behavior. Here are some of the most commonly used assertions:

- `self.assertEqual(a, b)`: Checks if `a` is equal to `b`.
- `self.assertNotEqual(a, b)`: Checks if `a` is not equal to `b`.
- `self.assertTrue(x)`: Checks if `x` is true.
- `self.assertFalse(x)`: Checks if `x` is false.
- `self.assertIs(a, b)`: Checks if `a` is the same object as `b`.
- `self.assertIsNot(a, b)`: Checks if `a` is not the same object as `b`.
- `self.assertIsNone(x)`: Checks if `x` is None.
- `self.assertIsNotNone(x)`: Checks if `x` is not None.
- `self.assertIn(a, b)`: Checks if `a` is in `b` (e.g., if a substring is in a string, or if an element is in a list).
- `self.assertNotIn(a, b)`: Checks if `a` is not in `b`.
- `self.assertIsInstance(a, b)`: Checks if `a` is an instance of class `b`.
- `self.assertNotIsInstance(a, b)`: Checks if `a` is not an instance of class `b`.
- `self.assertRaises(exc, fun, *args, **kwds)`: Checks if calling `fun(*args, **kwds)` raises exception `exc`.
- *
- `self.assertTemplateUsed(response, template_name)`: Checks if the template `template_name` was used to render the response.
- `self.assertContains(response, text, status_code=200, html=False)`: Checks if the response contains the given `text`.
- `self.assertNotContains(response, text, status_code=200, html=False)`: Checks if the response does not contain the given `text`.
-

3. Test Runner

Django's test runner is the command-line tool that you use to execute your tests. To run all the tests in your project, simply run the following command from your project's root directory (where manage.py is located):

Bash

```
python manage.py test
```

This will discover all the files that match the pattern test*.py in your apps and execute the tests defined within them.

You can also run specific tests:

- To run tests in a specific app:

Bash

```
python manage.py test myapp
```

- To run a specific test class:

Bash

```
python manage.py test myapp.ItemViewsTestCase
```

- To run a specific test method:

Bash

python manage.py test myapp.ItemViewsTestCase.test_item_list_view

Real-World Examples

- **E-commerce Website:** You might write tests to ensure that the shopping cart functionality works correctly, that product prices are calculated correctly, and that user orders are processed without errors.
- **Social Media Platform:** You might write tests to verify that users can create and delete posts, that user authentication works as expected, and that the news feed displays the correct information.
- **Content Management System (CMS):** You might write tests to ensure that articles can be created, edited, and published correctly, that user permissions are enforced, and that search functionality returns accurate results.

By using Django's testing tools effectively, you can write comprehensive tests that give you confidence in the quality and reliability of your web applications.

10.3 Test-Driven Development (TDD)

Test-Driven Development (TDD) is not just about writing tests; it's a development philosophy. It flips the traditional approach of writing code first and then writing tests to verify it. In TDD, you write the tests *before* you write the code.

The TDD Cycle

TDD follows a short, iterative cycle, often referred to as the "Red–Green–Refactor" cycle:

1. **Red:**
    - You start by writing a test that defines a small piece of functionality that you want to implement.
    - This test should fail initially because you haven't written the code to make it pass. This failing state is the "Red" state.
    - The test acts as a specification for the code you're about to write. It clearly defines what the code should do.

2. **Green:**
    - Next, you write the minimum amount of code necessary to make the failing test pass. You focus solely on getting the test to turn "Green" (pass).
    - You might write simple, even somewhat naive, code at this stage. The goal is to get the test passing quickly.

3. **Refactor:**
    - Once the test is green, you refactor your code. This means you improve its structure, design, and readability *without changing its behavior.*
    - You might clean up the code, remove duplication, improve variable names, etc.
    - Crucially, you run the tests again after refactoring. If the tests still pass, you can be confident that you haven't broken anything.

This cycle is repeated for each small piece of functionality you add to your application.

Benefits of TDD

- **Improved Code Design:** TDD encourages you to think about how your code will be used *before* you write it. This often leads to cleaner, more modular, and more maintainable code.
- **Reduced Bugs:** Because you're constantly writing tests, you're more likely to catch bugs early in the development process, when they are easier and cheaper to fix.
- **Increased Confidence:** TDD provides a safety net. When you refactor or add new features, you can run the tests to ensure that you haven't introduced any regressions (unintentional bugs).
- **Better Documentation:** Tests can serve as a form of documentation, illustrating how the code is intended to be used.
- **Focus:** TDD can help you stay focused on writing only the code that's needed. You avoid writing unnecessary code.

Example: TDD for a Simple String Reversal Function

Let's illustrate TDD with a very basic example: a function that reverses a string.

1. **Red:**
   - We start by writing a test for the simplest case: reversing an empty string.

Python

```python
import unittest
def reverse_string(s):
    pass  # Implementation comes later
class TestReverseString(unittest.TestCase):
    def test_reverse_empty_string(self):
self.assertEqual(reverse_string(""), "")
```

If you run this test, it will fail because reverse_string doesn't do anything yet.

2. **Green:**
   - Now, we write the minimum code to make this test pass.

Python

```python
def reverse_string(s):
return ""
```

This is a very basic implementation, but it makes the test pass.

3. **Refactor:**
   - There's not much to refactor yet.
4. **Red (Next Test):**

- Let's write a test for reversing a single-character string.

Python

```python
def test_reverse_single_character_string(self):
self.assertEqual(reverse_string("a"), "a")
```

This test will fail.

5. **Green:**
   - We update our code to pass this test.

Python

```python
def reverse_string(s):
return s
```

6. **Refactor:**
   - Still not much to refactor.
7. **Red (Next Test):**
   - Now, let's test reversing a two-character string.

Python

```python
def test_reverse_two_character_string(self):
```

self.assertEqual(reverse_string("ab"), "ba")

8. **Green:**
    - ○ We finally need to write the actual reversal logic.

Python

```python
def reverse_string(s):
 return s[::-1]  # Pythonic string reversa
```

9. **Refactor:**
    - ○ The code is now concise and readable.

We would continue this cycle, adding more tests for different scenarios (e.g., strings with spaces, palindromes, etc.) and refactoring as needed.

TDD in Django

You can apply TDD effectively in Django development. You would write tests for:

- **Models:** Ensuring model methods and properties behave correctly.
- **Views:** Verifying that views handle requests and return responses as expected.
- **Forms:** Testing form validation logic.
- **APIs:** Testing API endpoints and data serialization/deserialization.

Important Considerations

- **Learning Curve:** TDD has a learning curve. It requires practice and a shift in mindset.
- **Over-Testing:** Be careful not to over-test. Focus on testing the behavior of your code, not the implementation details.
- **Test Maintenance:** Tests need to be maintained along with your code. If you change the behavior of your code, you might need to update your tests.

TDD can significantly improve the quality of your code and make you a more effective developer. It's a valuable skill to learn and incorporate into your development workflow.

10.4 Debugging and Troubleshooting

Debugging is the process of identifying and removing errors (bugs) from your code.[1] Troubleshooting is a broader term that encompasses not only finding code errors but also diagnosing and resolving problems related to your application's environment, configuration, or dependencies.[2]

Debugging Tools and Techniques

Here are some essential tools and techniques for debugging Django applications:

1. **Django's Error Pages:**
   - When `DEBUG = True` in your `settings.py` (which it should be during development), Django

provides detailed error pages when an exception occurs.

- These pages include a traceback (the sequence of function calls that led to the error), the values of local variables, and other helpful information.[3]
- Learn to read tracebacks carefully. They are your primary guide to finding the source of the problem.

2. **Logging:**
   - Logging is a powerful tool for recording information about your application's behavior.[4]
   - You can log errors, warnings, informational messages, and even debug messages.[5]
   - Django provides a built-in logging framework that allows you to configure logging levels, formats, and output destinations (e.g., console, files).[6]

Python

```python
import logging
logger = logging.getLogger(__name__)  # Get a logger for the current module
def my_view(request):
    try:
        #  ... some code that might raise an exception ...
    except Exception as e:
        logger.error(f"An error occurred: {e}", exc_info=True)  # Log the error
        #  ... handle the error ...
```

- logging.getLogger(__name__): This gets a logger that is specific to the current module. This is a best practice as it makes it easier to trace where log messages originate.
- logger.error(): This logs an error message.
- exc_info=True: This adds traceback information to the log message.

3. **The Python Debugger (pdb):**
   - pdb is Python's built-in interactive source code debugger. It allows you to step through your code, set breakpoints, inspect variables, and execute code line by line.
   - You can insert breakpoints in your code using import pdb; pdb.set_trace(). When the code reaches this line, the debugger will start.

Python

```python
def my_function(x, y):
    import pdb; pdb.set_trace() # Start the debugger here
    result = x + y
    return result
```

- Once the debugger starts, you can use commands like:
  - n (next): Execute the next line of code.
  - s (step): Step into a function call.

- c (continue): Continue execution until the next breakpoint or the end of the program.[7]
- p variable_name: Print the value of a variable.
- pp variable_name: Pretty-print the value of a variable.
- q (quit): Quit the debugger.

4. **Browser Developer Tools:**
   - Modern web browsers have powerful developer tools that are essential for debugging front-end issues.[8]
   - These tools allow you to inspect HTML, CSS, and JavaScript, monitor network requests, and debug JavaScript code.
   - Pay attention to:
     - The "Console" tab: For JavaScript errors and logging.
     - The "Network" tab: For inspecting HTTP requests and responses (especially AJAX requests).[9]
     - The "Elements" tab: For inspecting HTML and CSS.[10]

5. **Django's** manage.py shell:
   - This command opens a Python shell with access to your Django project.
   - It's useful for inspecting data, testing code snippets, and interacting with your models.

Bash

python manage.py shell

Troubleshooting Common Django Issues

Here are some common issues you might encounter and how to approach them:

1. **Template Errors:**
   - **Symptom:** Your page doesn't render correctly, and you see errors related to template syntax or missing variables.
   - **Troubleshooting:**
     - Carefully review the traceback in the error page. It will tell you the exact line and file where the error occurred.
     - Double-check your template syntax (e.g., correct use of {{ variable }}, {% for %}, etc.).
     - Ensure that you're passing the correct data from your view to the template. Use pdb or logging to inspect the context data.
2. **Database Errors:**
   - **Symptom:** Your application fails to interact with the database, and you see errors related to SQL queries or database connections.[11]
   - **Troubleshooting:**
     - Check your settings.py file to ensure that your database configuration is correct (e.g., ENGINE, NAME, USER, PASSWORD).
     - Use python manage.py dbshell to connect to your database and execute SQL queries directly. This can help you diagnose issues with your database schema or data.

- Examine the SQL queries that Django is generating. You can enable logging of SQL queries in your settings.py for debugging.

3. **URL Resolution Errors:**
   - **Symptom:** You get NoReverseMatch errors when trying to generate URLs, or your links don't work correctly.
   - **Troubleshooting:**
     - Carefully review your urls.py files to ensure that your URL patterns are defined correctly and that you're using the correct names in your reverse() calls or template tags.
     - Use python manage.py show_urls to see a list of all your URL patterns.

4. **Form Validation Errors:**
   - **Symptom:** Your forms don't validate correctly, or you're not getting the expected error messages.
   - **Troubleshooting:**
     - Use pdb or logging to inspect the form.errors attribute in your view. This will show you the specific validation errors.
     - Double-check your form field definitions and validation logic.

5. **Static File Issues:**
   - **Symptom:** Your CSS, JavaScript, or images aren't loading correctly.
   - **Troubleshooting:**
     - Inspect the "Network" tab in your browser's developer tools to see if the

static files are being requested and if there are any errors.

- Ensure that your STATIC_URL and STATIC_ROOT settings are configured correctly in settings.py.
- Verify that your static files are located in the correct directories.

General Troubleshooting Tips

- **Read the Error Messages:** Error messages often provide valuable clues about the cause of the problem. Don't just dismiss them; read them carefully.
- **Isolate the Problem:** Try to narrow down the area of your code that's causing the issue.
- **Simplify:** If you're dealing with a complex problem, try to simplify it. Remove unnecessary code until you have a minimal example that reproduces the issue.
- **Use Version Control:** Use Git to track changes to your code.[12] This allows you to easily revert to previous versions if you introduce a bug.
- **Consult the Documentation:** Django's official documentation is an excellent resource for troubleshooting common problems.[13]
- **Search Online:** Search engines and online communities (like Stack Overflow) can be invaluable sources of information and solutions.

Debugging and troubleshooting can be challenging, but they are also essential skills for any developer. By using the right tools and techniques and by being patient and persistent, you can effectively solve even the most complex problems.

Chapter 11: Deployment Strategies

In this chapter, we'll explore the various ways to deploy your application to a production server. We'll cover preparing your app, choosing a hosting platform, setting up a database, configuring a web server, and even touch on Docker and CI/CD. Get ready to share your creations with the world!

11.1 Preparing Your Application for Deployment

Moving your Django application from your development environment to a production server involves more than just copying files. You need to configure it to handle real-world traffic, secure it against threats, and optimize its performance.

Here are the key steps to take before deploying your Django application:

1. Configure Settings for Production

Your settings.py file likely has settings that are suitable for development but not for production. You'll need to adjust these settings.

- DEBUG = False: This is perhaps the most important change. In development, DEBUG = True provides detailed error pages, which are helpful for debugging. However, in production, these error pages can expose sensitive information and should be turned off.

Python

DEBUG = False

- **ALLOWED_HOSTS**: This setting specifies a list of valid hostnames for your Django application. This is a crucial security measure to prevent HTTP Host header attacks. In development, you might have it set to ['*'] or ['localhost', '127.0.0.1']. In production, you *must* set it to the actual domain names or IP addresses that your application will be served from.

Python

ALLOWED_HOSTS = ['yourdomain.com', 'www.yourdomain.com', '192.168.1.10']

- **SECRET_KEY**: This setting is used for cryptographic signing and should be kept secret. In development, you might use a simple string. In production, you should generate a strong, random, and complex secret key and store it securely (e.g., as an environment variable).

Python

```python
import os
SECRET_KEY = os.environ.get('DJANGO_SECRET_KEY', 'your_default_secret_key')
```

- **DATABASES**: Ensure your database settings are correct for your production database. This will likely involve changing the ENGINE, NAME, USER, PASSWORD, HOST, and PORT settings.

Python

```python
DATABASES = {
  'default': {
    'ENGINE': 'django.db.backends.postgresql',
    'NAME': 'mydatabase',
    'USER': 'myuser',
    'PASSWORD': 'mypassword',
    'HOST': 'myhost',
    'PORT': '5432',
  }
}
```

- **STATIC_ROOT** and STATIC_URL: These settings are important for serving static files (CSS, JavaScript, images). STATIC_URL is the base URL for your static files (e.g., /static/). STATIC_ROOT is the absolute path to the directory where you'll collect all your static files for production serving.

Python

import os

```python
from pathlib import Path
BASE_DIR = Path(__file__).resolve().parent.parent  # Usually
defined by Django
STATIC_URL = '/static/'
STATIC_ROOT = os.path.join(BASE_DIR, 'staticfiles')
```

- MEDIA_ROOT **and** MEDIA_URL: If your application handles user-uploaded files (e.g., profile pictures), you'll also need MEDIA_ROOT (the directory where uploaded files are stored) and MEDIA_URL (the base URL for serving uploaded files).

Python

```python
MEDIA_URL = '/media/'
MEDIA_ROOT = os.path.join(BASE_DIR, 'media')
```

2. Collect Static Files

In development, Django can serve static files. However, in production, it's more efficient to have your web server (Nginx, Apache) serve them directly.

To prepare for this, you need to collect all your static files into the STATIC_ROOT directory. Run the following command:

Bash

```bash
python manage.py collectstatic
```

This command will copy all the static files from your apps' static directories and any other directories specified in STATICFILES_DIRS to the STATIC_ROOT directory.

3. Security Best Practices

Security is paramount in production. Here are some key practices:

- **HTTPS:** Use HTTPS to encrypt communication between the browser and the server. This prevents eavesdropping and man-in-the-middle attacks. You'll need to obtain an SSL certificate and configure your web server to use it.
- **CSRF Protection:** Django provides built-in protection against Cross-Site Request Forgery (CSRF) attacks. Ensure that you're using the {% csrf_token %} template tag in all your forms that use the POST method.
- **Security Middleware:** Django's SecurityMiddleware provides various security enhancements. Ensure it's included in your MIDDLEWARE setting.

Python

```
MIDDLEWARE = [
    # ...
    'django.middleware.security.SecurityMiddleware',
    # ...
]
```

- **Secure Headers:** Consider setting security-related HTTP headers to further enhance security. SecurityMiddleware can help with some of these.
- **Regular Updates:** Keep your Django version, Python version, and all your dependencies up to date to patch security vulnerabilities.
- **Input Validation:** Always validate user input on the server-side to prevent vulnerabilities like SQL injection and XSS.

4. Check for Dependencies

Make sure you have a requirements.txt file that lists all the Python packages your application depends on. This ensures that you can easily recreate your environment on the production server.

Bash

pip freeze > requirements.txt

5. Testing

Thoroughly test your application in a staging environment (a production-like environment) before deploying to production. This helps catch any issues that might only appear in a production setting.

Real-World Example

Let's say you're deploying an e-commerce website.

- You'd set ALLOWED_HOSTS to your domain name (e.g., ['shop.example.com']).

- You'd use a strong, randomly generated SECRET_KEY stored securely on your server.
- You'd configure your database to use a production-ready database like PostgreSQL.
- You'd collect your static files and configure your web server to serve them efficiently.
- You'd obtain an SSL certificate and configure HTTPS.
- You'd test the entire checkout process and all other critical functionality in a staging environment before making the site live.

By carefully preparing your application for deployment, you can ensure a smooth, secure, and reliable experience for your users.

11.2 Choosing a Hosting Platform

There's no one-size-fits-all answer to where you should host your Django application. The best choice depends on factors like your application's complexity, traffic volume, budget, and technical expertise.

Here's a breakdown of some common hosting options:

1. Platform as a Service (PaaS)

- **What it is:** PaaS providers like Heroku, PythonAnywhere, and Google App Engine offer a managed hosting environment. They handle much of the underlying infrastructure, allowing you to focus primarily on your application code.

- **Pros:**
  - ○ **Ease of Use:** PaaS platforms are generally very easy to set up and deploy to. They automate many server configuration tasks.
  - ○ **Scalability:** PaaS platforms often provide built-in scaling features, allowing your application to handle increased traffic.
  - ○ **Reduced Maintenance:** The PaaS provider handles server maintenance, security updates, and other infrastructure tasks.
  - ○ **Faster Development:** PaaS platforms can speed up the development and deployment process.
- **Cons:**
  - ○ **Less Control:** You have less control over the server environment compared to IaaS.
  - ○ **Vendor Lock-in:** You might be tied to the specific PaaS platform's ecosystem.
  - ○ **Cost:** PaaS can become more expensive than IaaS as your application scales.
- **Example: Heroku**
  - ○ Heroku is a popular PaaS that makes deploying Django applications relatively straightforward.
  - ○ You typically use a Procfile to define how your application should be run and deploy using the Heroku CLI (Command Line Interface).
  - ○ Heroku provides add-ons for databases, caching, and other services.

2. Infrastructure as a Service (IaaS)

- **What it is:** IaaS providers like Amazon Web Services (AWS), Google Cloud Platform (GCP), and DigitalOcean provide virtual servers (in the cloud) that you manage yourself.
- **Pros:**
  - **More Control:** You have full control over the server environment, allowing you to customize it to your needs.
  - **Flexibility:** You can choose the operating system, web server, database, and other software.
  - **Cost-Effective (Potentially):** IaaS can be more cost-effective than PaaS for large-scale applications.
- **Cons:**
  - **More Complex:** You're responsible for server configuration, security, and maintenance.
  - **Steeper Learning Curve:** IaaS requires more technical expertise.
  - **More Time Investment:** Setting up and managing IaaS infrastructure takes more time.
- **Examples:**
  - **AWS (Amazon Web Services):**
    - AWS offers a wide range of services, including EC2 (virtual servers), RDS (managed databases), and S3 (storage).
    - Deploying Django on AWS involves setting up EC2 instances, configuring a web server (Nginx, Apache), setting up a database (RDS), and managing security.
  - **DigitalOcean:**
    - DigitalOcean provides virtual servers ("Droplets") that are easy to set up.

- It's a good option for developers who want more control than PaaS but don't need the complexity of AWS.

3. Other Options

- **Traditional Hosting:** Shared hosting or VPS (Virtual Private Server) from traditional hosting providers. These can be cost-effective for very simple applications but often lack the scalability and flexibility of PaaS and IaaS.

Choosing the Right Platform

Here's a guide to help you decide:

- **Small Projects/Beginners:** PaaS (Heroku, PythonAnywhere) is often a good choice for small projects or beginners due to its ease of use.
- **Medium-Sized Projects/Growing Applications:** IaaS (DigitalOcean) can provide a good balance of control and cost-effectiveness.
- **Large-Scale/Complex Applications:** IaaS (AWS, GCP) offers the scalability and flexibility needed for large, complex applications, but requires more expertise.

Important Considerations

- **Scalability:** How easily can the platform handle increased traffic and data?
- **Cost:** Consider both the initial cost and the cost as your application grows.

- **Maintenance:** How much responsibility are you willing to take for server maintenance?
- **Security:** Does the platform provide adequate security features?
- **Support:** What level of support is available from the provider?
- **Database:** Does the platform easily integrate with your preferred database (PostgreSQL, MySQL)?
- **Deployment Workflow:** How easy is it to deploy and update your application?
- **Monitoring and Logging:** Does the platform provide tools for monitoring your application's performance and logging errors?

No Code Example

Since this chapter is about *choosing* a platform, there isn't specific code to provide. The "code" is in the configuration and setup you'll do *on* the chosen platform, which varies significantly.

Real-World Examples

- A simple personal blog might be hosted on PythonAnywhere or a basic DigitalOcean Droplet.
- A growing e-commerce startup might start on Heroku and then migrate to AWS as its needs become more complex.
- A large enterprise application with high availability requirements would likely be hosted on a robust IaaS platform like AWS or GCP.

Choosing the right hosting platform is a critical decision that will impact your application's success. Carefully consider your needs and priorities before making your choice.

11.3 Setting Up a Production Database (PostgreSQL, MySQL)

Why not SQLite in production?

- **Concurrency:** SQLite is designed for single-user access. It doesn't handle concurrent connections well, which is crucial for a web application serving multiple users.
- **Performance:** PostgreSQL and MySQL are generally faster and more efficient for complex queries and large datasets.
- **Scalability:** PostgreSQL and MySQL are designed to scale to handle high traffic and large amounts of data.[1]
- **Features:** PostgreSQL and MySQL offer more advanced features, such as transactions, stored procedures, and more sophisticated data types.[2]

Choosing Between PostgreSQL and MySQL

Both PostgreSQL and MySQL are excellent choices for production databases. Here's a brief comparison:

- **PostgreSQL:**
  - Strong adherence to SQL standards.
  - Advanced features, such as complex queries, data integrity, and extensibility.
  - Known for its reliability and robustness.

- Often preferred for applications with complex data requirements.
- **MySQL:**
  - Widely used and has a large community.
  - Good performance for many web applications.
  - Can be easier to set up and configure in some cases.
  - Often a good choice for web applications with standard data needs.

For this explanation, let's focus on PostgreSQL, as it's often favored for Django applications due to its strong features and reliability.

Setting Up PostgreSQL

Here's a general guide to setting up PostgreSQL for production:

1. **Install PostgreSQL:**
   - The installation process varies depending on your operating system.
   - On Linux (Debian/Ubuntu):

Bash

```
sudo apt-get update
sudo apt-get install postgresql postgresql-contrib
```

- On macOS (using Homebrew):

Bash

brew install postgresql

On Windows, download the installer from the official PostgreSQL website.[3]

2. **Create a Database and User:**
   - After installation, you'll need to create a database and a user that your Django application will use.
   - You can do this using the PostgreSQL command-line tools.[4]

Bash

sudo -u postgres psql # Log in as the 'postgres' user

- Inside the psql shell:

SQL

```
CREATE DATABASE mydatabase;
CREATE USER myuser WITH PASSWORD 'mypassword';
GRANT ALL PRIVILEGES ON DATABASE mydatabase TO
myuser;
\q  # Exit psql
```

- Replace mydatabase, myuser, and mypassword with your desired names and password.
- GRANT ALL PRIVILEGES gives the user full access to the database. You might want to restrict privileges further in a production environment for security.

3. **Configure Django Settings:**
   ○ In your Django project's settings.py file, configure the DATABASES setting to connect to your PostgreSQL database.

```
DATABASES = {

'default': {

'ENGINE': 'django.db.backends.postgresql',

'NAME': 'mydatabase',

'USER': 'myuser',

'PASSWORD': 'mypassword',

'HOST': 'localhost',5 # Or the hostname of your database
server
```

'PORT': '5432', # Default PostgreSQL port

```
}

}
```

```
```

Ensure that these settings match the database name, user, password, host, and port you configured in PostgreSQL.

4. **Install** psycopg2:
   ○ Django uses the psycopg2 library to communicate with PostgreSQL. You'll need to install it in your Django project's virtual environment.

Bash

pip install psycopg2-binary   # Or psycopg2 (see notes below)

■ **Important Note:** psycopg2-binary is a convenient way to get started, as it includes pre-compiled binaries. However, for production, it's generally recommended to install the regular psycopg2 package, as it can offer better performance and stability. You might need to install PostgreSQL development libraries on your system to compile psycopg2.

5. **Run Migrations:**
   - After configuring your database settings, you need to apply the initial database migrations to create the necessary tables.

Bash

```
python manage.py migrate
```

Security Considerations

- **Strong Passwords:** Use strong, unique passwords for your database user.
- **Firewall:** Configure your server's firewall to allow only necessary connections to the PostgreSQL port (5432 by default).[6]
- **Network Isolation:** If possible, keep your database server on a separate, isolated network from your web server.
- **Principle of Least Privilege:** Grant your Django database user only the necessary privileges. Avoid granting SUPERUSER privileges.
- **Regular Backups:** Implement a robust backup strategy to protect your data from loss.

Real-World Example

Let's say you're deploying an e-commerce application.

- You would set up a dedicated PostgreSQL server to handle the large volume of product data, user orders, and transaction information.
- You would carefully configure the database settings in your Django application to ensure a reliable connection.
- You would implement regular database backups to protect against data loss in case of server failure.
- You would secure the database server by configuring firewall rules and restricting access to authorized users only.

By following these steps and considering security best practices, you can set up a production-ready PostgreSQL database for your Django application, ensuring data integrity, performance, and security.

11.4 Configuring a Web Server (Nginx, Apache)

A web server is responsible for receiving HTTP requests from clients (like web browsers) and serving the appropriate responses. For Django applications, the web server doesn't directly execute your Python code. Instead, it typically passes requests to a WSGI server, which then interacts with your Django application.

Understanding WSGI

WSGI (Web Server Gateway Interface) is a standard interface between web servers and Python web applications. It allows different web servers to communicate with Django (or any other Python web framework) in a consistent way.

Choosing Between Nginx and Apache

Both Nginx and Apache are robust and widely used web servers. Here's a brief comparison:

- **Nginx:**
    - Known for its high performance and efficiency, especially for serving static content and handling concurrent connections.
    - Uses an asynchronous, event-driven architecture.
    - Often preferred for high-traffic websites and applications.
- **Apache:**
    - A versatile and highly configurable web server.
    - Uses a process-based or thread-based architecture.
    - Offers a wide range of modules for various functionalities.

For Django applications, Nginx is often recommended due to its performance and efficiency, especially when serving static files. Therefore, we'll focus on Nginx in this explanation.

Setting Up Nginx for Django

Here's a general guide to setting up Nginx to serve your Django application:

1. **Install Nginx:**
   - The installation process varies depending on your operating system.
   - On Linux (Debian/Ubuntu):

Bash

```
sudo apt-get update
sudo apt-get install nginx
```

   - On macOS (using Homebrew):

Bash

```
brew install nginx
```

On Windows, download the installer from the official Nginx website.

2. **Install a WSGI Server:**
   - As mentioned earlier, Nginx needs to communicate with your Django application through a WSGI server. Gunicorn and uWSGI are popular choices. Let's use Gunicorn.

Bash

pip install gunicorn

3. **Configure Gunicorn:**
   - You can run Gunicorn to serve your Django project.
   - From your project's root directory (where manage.py is located):

Bash

gunicorn myproject.wsgi:application --bind 0.0.0.0:8000

   - Replace myproject with the name of your project.
   - myproject.wsgi:application tells Gunicorn where to find your WSGI application.
   - --bind 0.0.0.0:8000 tells Gunicorn to listen on all interfaces (0.0.0.0) and port 8000.
   - You might want to use a different port if 8000 is occupied.

4. **Configure Nginx:**
   - You need to configure Nginx to act as a reverse proxy, passing requests to Gunicorn and serving static files directly.

- Nginx configuration files are usually located in /etc/nginx/nginx.conf or in a site-specific configuration directory like /etc/nginx/sites-available/.
- Create a configuration file for your Django project (e.g., /etc/nginx/sites-available/myproject).

Nginx

```
server {
  listen 80;
   server_name yourdomain.com www.yourdomain.com;  # Replace with your domain names
  access_log /var/log/nginx/myproject_access.log;
  error_log /var/log/nginx/myproject_error.log;
  location / {
      proxy_pass http://127.0.0.1:8000;  # Pass requests to Gunicorn
    proxy_set_header Host $host;
    proxy_set_header X-Real-IP $remote_addr;
            proxy_set_header   X-Forwarded-For $proxy_add_x_forwarded_for;
    proxy_set_header X-Forwarded-Proto $scheme;
  }
  location /static/ {
     alias /path/to/your/staticfiles/;  # Replace with the path to your STATIC_ROOT
  }
```

```
location /media/ {
    alias /path/to/your/mediafiles/;  # Replace with the path
to your MEDIA_ROOT (if applicable)
    }
}
```

- listen 80;: Tells Nginx to listen on port 80
  (the default HTTP port).
- server_name yourdomain.com
  www.yourdomain.com;: Specifies the
  domain names that this server block
  should handle.
- access_log and error_log: Define where to
  store access and error logs.
- location / { ... }: This block handles all
  requests to the root URL (/).
  - proxy_pass http://127.0.0.1:8000;:
    Passes requests to Gunicorn, which
    is running on localhost port 8000.
  - proxy_set_header ...: Sets headers to
    pass information about the original
    request to Gunicorn.
- location /static/ { ... }: This block handles
  requests to URLs starting with /static/.
  - alias /path/to/your/staticfiles/;:
    Tells Nginx where to find your static
    files (replace
    /path/to/your/staticfiles/ with the
    actual path to your STATIC_ROOT
    directory).

- location /media/ { ... }: This block is similar to /static/ but handles user-uploaded media files (if applicable).

5. **Enable the Configuration:**
   - Create a symbolic link from the configuration file in /etc/nginx/sites-available/ to /etc/nginx/sites-enabled/.

Bash

```
sudo ln -s /etc/nginx/sites-available/myproject /etc/nginx/sites-enabled/myproject
```

6. **Restart Nginx:**

Bash

```
sudo systemctl restart nginx
```

Important Considerations

- **Security:** Configure firewalls to allow only necessary traffic to your server. Use HTTPS to encrypt communication.
- **Performance:** Optimize Nginx and Gunicorn settings for performance. Consider caching static files.
- **Logging:** Pay attention to your web server logs for errors and troubleshooting.

- **Supervision:** Use a process manager (like systemd or Supervisor) to ensure Gunicorn is always running.

Real-World Example

Let's say you're deploying a social media application.

- You'd set up Nginx to handle a high volume of requests efficiently.
- You'd configure Nginx to serve static assets (images, CSS, JavaScript) directly, reducing the load on your Django application.
- You'd use Gunicorn to serve your Django application, scaling the number of Gunicorn workers based on traffic.
- You'd configure logging to monitor the application's performance and identify any errors.

By correctly configuring your web server, you can ensure that your Django application is served efficiently, securely, and reliably.

11.5 Deploying with Docker and Containerization (Optional)

Docker is a platform that allows you to package your application and its dependencies into a standardized unit called a container.[1] Containerization[2] is the process of packaging software in this way.[3]

Think of a container like a lightweight virtual machine. It contains everything your application needs to run: code, runtime, system tools, system libraries, and settings.[4]

Benefits of Using Docker

- **Consistency:** Docker ensures that your application runs the same way in any environment, whether it's your development machine, a testing server, or a production server.[5] This eliminates "it works on my machine" issues.[6]
- **Portability:** You can easily move containers between different machines or cloud providers.[7]
- **Isolation:** Containers provide isolation, preventing your application from interfering with other applications on the same server, and vice versa.[8]
- **Scalability:** Docker makes it easier to scale your application by running multiple containers.[9]
- **Faster Deployment:** Docker can speed up deployment by automating the process of building and deploying containers.[10]

Docker Concepts

- **Image:** A Docker image is a read-only template that contains instructions for creating a container.[11] It's like a blueprint.
- **Container:** A running instance of an image. It's the actual running application.
- **Dockerfile:** A text file that contains the instructions for building a Docker image.[12]
- **Docker Compose:** A tool for defining and running multi-container Docker applications.[1314]

Deploying a Django Application with Docker

Here's a general workflow for deploying a Django application with Docker:

1. **Create a Dockerfile:**
   - This file defines how to build your Docker image.[15]

Dockerfile

```
# Use an official Python runtime as a parent image
FROM python:3.9-slim-buster
# Set environment variables
ENV PYTHONDONTWRITEBYTECODE 1
ENV PYTHONUNBUFFERED 1
# Set the working directory in the container
WORKDIR /app
# Copy the current directory contents into the container at /app
COPY . /app
# Install system dependencies (if any)
# RUN apt-get update && apt-get install -y --no-install-recommends ...
# Install Python dependencies
RUN pip install --no-cache-dir -r requirements.txt
# Expose port 8000 for the Django application
EXPOSE 8000
# Run Gunicorn when the container starts
CMD ["gunicorn", "myproject.wsgi:application", "--bind", "0.0.0.0:8000"]
```

- FROM: Specifies the base image to use (a Python image in this case).
- ENV: Sets environment variables.
- WORKDIR: Sets the working directory inside the container.
- COPY: Copies files from your machine to the container.
- RUN: Executes commands inside the container (e.g., installing dependencies).
- EXPOSE: Exposes a port so the application can be accessed from outside the container.
- CMD: Specifies the command to run when the container starts (in this case, running Gunicorn).

2. **Create a** requirements.txt **File:**
   - List all your Python dependencies.

Bash

```
pip freeze > requirements.txt
```

3. **Build the Docker Image:**
   - From the directory containing your Dockerfile, run:

Bash

```
docker build -t my-django-app .
```

- o -t **my-django-app**: Tags the image with the name "my-django-app".
- o .: Specifies the current directory as the build context.
4. **Run the Docker Container:**
   - o Run the image to create a container:

Bash

```
docker run -p 8000:8000 my-django-app
```

- o -p 8000:8000: Maps port 8000 on your machine to port 8000 inside the container. You can now access your Django application in your browser at http://localhost:8000.
5. **Use Docker Compose (for multi-container apps):**
   - o If your application involves multiple services (e.g., a web application and a database), Docker Compose can help you manage them.[16]
   - o Create a docker-compose.yml file:

YAML

```
version: "3.9"  # Or a compatible Docker Compose version
services:
  web:
```

```yaml
    build: .  #   Build the web service from the current
directory
  ports:
   - "8000:8000"
  depends_on:
     - db  #   The web service depends on the database
service
  db:
       image:  postgres:13-alpine  #    Use the official
PostgreSQL image
    volumes:
     - db_data:/var/lib/postgresql/data  #  Persist database
data
    environment:
     POSTGRES_USER: myuser
     POSTGRES_PASSWORD: mypassword
     POSTGRES_DB: mydatabase
  volumes:
   db_data:  #  Define the volume for database data
```

○ Run the application with Docker Compose:

Bash

```bash
docker-compose up -d  #   -d runs the services in detached
mode (background)
```

Important Considerations

316

- **Optimization:** Optimize your Docker images for size and performance.[17] Use multi-stage builds, minimize layers, and choose efficient base images.[18]
- **Security:** Secure your Docker containers and the host system.[19] Follow Docker security best practices.
- **Orchestration:** For large-scale deployments, consider using container orchestration tools like Kubernetes or Docker Swarm to manage and scale your containers.[20]
- **Volumes:** Use volumes to persist data that needs to survive container restarts (e.g., database data).[21]
- **Networking:** Understand Docker networking to allow your containers to communicate with each other.[22]

Real-World Example

Let's say you're deploying a complex web application with a Django backend, a PostgreSQL database, and a Redis cache.

- You would use Docker Compose to define and run these services as separate containers.[23]
- Docker would ensure that each service has its dependencies and configurations, regardless of the deployment environment.[24]
- You could easily scale your application by running more containers of the Django backend.
- You could deploy the entire application to different cloud providers with minimal changes.

Docker and containerization provide a powerful and flexible way to deploy Django applications, especially for complex and scalable projects.

11.6 Using CI/CD Pipelines

CI/CD stands for Continuous Integration/Continuous Delivery or Continuous Deployment. It's a set of practices designed to automate the software development lifecycle, from code changes to deployment.

Why Use CI/CD?

- **Faster Releases:** Automating the process allows you to release new features and bug fixes more frequently.
- **Reduced Errors:** Automated testing and deployment steps help catch errors early and prevent them from reaching production.
- **Increased Efficiency:** Developers can focus on writing code instead of spending time on manual deployment tasks.
- **Improved Quality:** Automated testing ensures that code changes don't break existing functionality.
- **Rollback Capabilities:** In case of a problem, CI/CD pipelines often make it easier to rollback to a previous working version.

Key Concepts

- **Continuous Integration (CI):** This practice focuses on automating the integration of code changes from multiple developers into a shared repository.
  - Developers frequently commit their code changes.
  - Each commit triggers an automated build and test process.

- This process verifies that the changes don't introduce errors or conflicts.
- **Continuous Delivery (CD):** This practice extends CI by automating the release of validated code to a staging or production environment.
  - Automated deployment pipelines deploy code to different environments.
  - This enables faster and more reliable releases.
- **Continuous Deployment (CD):** This is a more advanced practice where every code change that passes the automated tests is automatically deployed to production.
  - This requires a high degree of automation and confidence in the testing process.

CI/CD Pipeline Stages

A typical CI/CD pipeline consists of several stages:

1. **Source:** This stage monitors the source code repository (e.g., Git) for changes.
2. **Build:** This stage compiles the code, installs dependencies, and creates deployable artifacts (e.g., Docker images).
3. **Test:** This stage runs automated tests to verify the code's functionality.
4. **Deploy:** This stage deploys the artifacts to a target environment (e.g., staging, production).

Tools for CI/CD

There are many tools available for implementing CI/CD. Some popular options include:

- **Jenkins:** A widely used open-source automation server.
- **GitLab CI/CD:** CI/CD tools integrated into GitLab.
- **GitHub Actions:** CI/CD tools integrated into GitHub.
- **CircleCI:** A cloud-based CI/CD platform.
- **Travis CI:** Another cloud-based CI/CD platform.
- **Azure DevOps:** CI/CD tools from Microsoft.

Example: Setting Up a Basic CI/CD Pipeline with GitHub Actions

Let's look at a very basic example of setting up a CI/CD pipeline using GitHub Actions to run tests.

1. **Project Setup:**
   - Assume you have a Django project with tests.
2. **Create a GitHub Repository:**
   - Host your Django project on GitHub.
3. **Create a GitHub Actions Workflow File:**
   - In your project's root directory, create a directory named .github/workflows.
   - Inside the workflows directory, create a YAML file (e.g., django-ci.yml) to define your workflow.

YAML

```
name: Django CI
on:
 push:
 branches: [ "main" ]
```

```
  pull_request:
  branches: [ "main" ]
jobs:
 build:
  runs-on: ubuntu-latest
  steps:
    - uses: actions/checkout@v3
    - name: Set up Python 3.9
     uses: actions/setup-python@v4
     with:
      python-version: "3.9"
    - name: Install Dependencies
     run: |
      python -m pip install --upgrade pip
      pip install -r requirements.txt
    - name: Run Tests
     run: |
      python manage.py test
```

- ○ name: The name of the workflow.
- ○ on: Specifies when the workflow should run. In this case, it runs on every push to the main branch and on every pull request to the main branch.
- ○ jobs: Defines the jobs to be executed.
  - ■ build: The name of the job.
  - ■ runs-on: Specifies the runner environment (in this case, Ubuntu).
  - ■ steps: Defines the sequence of steps to be executed.
    - ■ actions/checkout@v3: Checks out the code from the repository.

- **actions/setup-python@v4**: Sets up Python 3.9.
- **Install Dependencies**: Installs the required Python packages from requirements.txt.
- **Run Tests**: Executes the Django tests using python manage.py test.

4. **Commit and Push:**
   - Commit and push the .github/workflows/django-ci.yml file to your GitHub repository.

Now, every time you push code to the main branch or create a pull request to it, GitHub Actions will automatically:

- Checkout your code.
- Set up Python.
- Install your project's dependencies.
- Run your Django tests.

If the tests pass, the workflow will succeed; otherwise, it will fail, indicating a problem with your code.

Important Considerations

- **Testing:** Writing comprehensive tests is crucial for successful CI/CD. Your pipeline's effectiveness depends on the quality of your tests.
- **Deployment Strategy:** Choose a deployment strategy that suits your needs (e.g., blue/green deployment, rolling deployment).

- **Security:** Secure your CI/CD pipeline to prevent unauthorized access and code changes.
- **Monitoring:** Implement monitoring to track your application's performance and identify issues after deployment.

CI/CD is a powerful practice that can significantly improve your software development process. By automating your releases, you can deliver high-quality software faster and more reliably.

Chapter 12: Performance Optimization and Security

In this chapter, we're going to explore how to optimize performance and secure your applications from common threats. We'll learn about caching, database optimization, security best practices, monitoring, and scalability. Get ready to build applications that are both fast and secure!

12.1 Caching Strategies

In web applications, many requests involve retrieving the same data repeatedly. For example:

- A product detail page might be accessed by many users.
- A list of recent blog posts might be displayed on multiple pages.
- The results of a complex database query might be needed frequently.

Instead of re-calculating or re-fetching this data every time, you can store it in a cache. When a request comes in, you first check if the data is in the cache. If it is (a "cache hit"), you serve the data from the cache, which is much faster. If it's not (a "cache miss"), you retrieve the data from the original source, store it in the cache, and then serve it.

Levels of Caching in Django

Django provides several levels of caching, allowing you to fine-tune your caching strategy:

1. **Per-Site Cache:**
   - This is the simplest form of caching. You cache the entire output of a view.
   - It's useful for pages that don't change frequently and are the same for all users.
   - To use per-site caching, you **add** 'django.middleware.cache.UpdateCacheMiddle ware' **and** 'django.middleware.cache.FetchFromCacheMid dleware' **to your** MIDDLEWARE[1] setting in settings.py. The order is important: UpdateCacheMiddleware must come first, and FetchFromCacheMiddleware must come last.

Python

```
MIDDLEWARE = [
    'django.middleware.cache.UpdateCacheMiddleware',
    'django.middleware.security.SecurityMiddleware',
    'django.contrib.sessions.middleware.SessionMiddleware',
    'django.middleware.common.CommonMiddleware',
    'django.middleware.csrf.CsrfViewMiddleware',

'django.contrib.auth.middleware.AuthenticationMiddleware
',

'django.contrib.messages.middleware.MessageMiddleware',
```

'django.middleware.clickjacking.XFrameOptionsMiddlewar
e',
  'django.middleware.cache.FetchFromCacheMiddleware',
]

CACHE_MIDDLEWARE_ALIAS = 'default'   #   Which cache
alias to use
CACHE_MIDDLEWARE_SECONDS = 600   #   How long to
cache pages for
CACHE_MIDDLEWARE_KEY_PREFIX = '' # Should start with
empty string. Don't use a slash (/)

- o You also need to configure a cache backend (see
    below).
- o This approach caches the entire HTML response.
2. **Per-View Cache:**
    - o This allows you to cache the output of individual
      views.
    - o It's more flexible than per-site caching, as you
      can choose which views to cache.
    - o You use the cache_page decorator to cache a
      view:

Python

from django.views.decorators.cache import cache_page
from django.shortcuts import render
@cache_page(60 * 15) # Cache the view for 15 minutes

```
def my_view(request):
    #  ... your view logic ...
        return render(request, 'my_template.html', {'data':
my_data})
```

cache_page takes the cache timeout in seconds as an argument.

3. **Template Fragment Caching:**
   - This allows you to cache specific parts of a template.
   - It's useful for caching complex or expensive-to-generate parts of a page, while still allowing other parts to be dynamic.
   - You use the {% cache %} template tag:

HTML

```
{% load cache %}
{% cache 600 my_fragment_cache_key %}
  {#  This part of the template will be cached for 10 minutes #}
  {#  ... expensive template code ... #}
{% endcache %}
```

   - **600** is the cache timeout in seconds.

- my_fragment_cache_key is a unique name for this cache fragment. You can use variables to make the key dynamic.

4. **Database Caching:**
   - This is the most fine-grained level of caching. You cache the results of database queries.
   - Django's ORM doesn't provide built-in database query caching, but you can achieve it using techniques like:
     - Caching the results of querysets in your own code.
     - Using a caching database backend (if available).
     - Using a database-level caching mechanism (e.g., PostgreSQL's query cache).

Cache Backends

Django supports several cache backends:

- **Memory Caching:**
  - Stores data in the server's memory.
  - Fastest option, but data is lost when the server restarts.
  - Suitable for development or small-scale applications.
  - To use memory caching:

Python

```
CACHES = {
'default': {
'BACKEND':
'django.core.cache.backends.locmem.LocMemCache',
 }
}
```

- **File System Caching:**
  - Stores data in files on the server's file system.
  - Slower than memory caching, but data persists across restarts.
  - Suitable for applications where data persistence is important but performance is less critical.
  - To use file system caching:

Python

```
CACHES = {
  'default': {
                                          'BACKEND':
'django.core.cache.backends.filebased.FileBasedCache',
  'LOCATION': '/var/tmp/django_cache', #  Replace with your
desired cache location
  }
}
```

- **Memcached:**
  - A high-performance, distributed memory object caching system.

- Very fast and scalable.
- Data is lost when the server restarts.
- Suitable for large-scale applications where performance is critical.
- Requires installing the python-memcached or pylibmc Python library and a Memcached server.
- To use Memcached:

Python

```
CACHES = {
  'default': {
                                    'BACKEND':
'django.core.cache.backends.memcached.PyMemcacheCach
e',                    #                    or
'django.core.cache.backends.memcached.MemcachedCache'
    'LOCATION': '127.0.0.1:11211',  #  Replace with your
Memcached server address
  }
}
```

- **Redis:**
  - An in-memory data structure store, used as a database, cache and message broker.
  - Very fast and offers data persistence.
  - Highly versatile and scalable.
  - Requires installing the django-redis Python library and a Redis server.
  - To use Redis:

Python

```
CACHES = {
'default': {
'BACKEND': 'django_redis.cache.RedisCache',
 'LOCATION': 'redis://127.0.0.1:6379/1',  #   Replace with your
Redis server address
 'OPTIONS': {
'CLIENT_CLASS': 'django_redis.client.DefaultClient',
 }
 }
}
```

- **Database Caching:**
  - Stores cached data in your database.
  - Slowest option, but data persists across restarts.
  - Generally not recommended for high-performance applications.
  - To use database caching:

Python

```
CACHES = {
'default': {
'BACKEND':
'django.core.cache.backends.db.DatabaseCache',
```

```
'LOCATION': 'my_cache_table',  #  Replace with your desired
cache table name
  }
}
```

- You'll need to create the cache table using
  python manage.py createcachetable.

Choosing the Right Caching Strategy

- **Per-site caching:** Use for simple sites with mostly static content.
- **Per-view caching:** A good balance of flexibility and performance improvement.
- **Template fragment caching:** Use for complex pages with parts that are expensive to generate.
- **Database caching:** Use only if data persistence is absolutely critical and performance is not a primary concern.

Real-World Examples

- **E-commerce Website:**
  - Cache product details, category pages, and search results.
  - Use a high-performance backend like Redis or Memcached.
- **News Website:**
  - Cache articles, front pages, and popular articles.
  - Use template fragment caching to cache parts of the page, such as the comment section.

- **Social Media Platform:**
    - Cache user profiles, timelines, and search results.
    - Consider using a distributed cache system for scalability.

By implementing effective caching strategies, you can significantly improve the performance and responsiveness of your Django applications, providing a better user experience and reducing server load.

12.2 Database Optimization

Database interactions can be a significant bottleneck in web applications.[2] If your queries are slow or your database is not structured efficiently, it can lead to sluggish response times and a poor user experience.[3] Django's ORM (Object-Relational Mapper) is powerful, but it's important to use it wisely to avoid performance problems.

Here are some key areas to focus on when optimizing your database interactions in Django:

1. Query Optimization

Writing efficient database queries is crucial. Django's ORM provides several tools to help you with this.[4]

- select_related(): This method is used to retrieve related objects in a single database query.[5] It's particularly useful for ForeignKey relationships.[6]

Python

```
#  Inefficient: Multiple queries
for book in Book.objects.all():
   print(book.author.name) #  One query per book
#  Efficient: Single query
for book in Book.objects.select_related('author').all():
   print(book.author.name)
```

- o In the inefficient example, a separate database query is executed for each book to retrieve the author's name.
- o select_related('author') fetches the author data along with the book data in a single query, significantly improving performance.
- prefetch_related(): This method is similar to select_related(), but it's used for ManyToManyField and reverse ForeignKey relationships. It uses a separate query for each relationship and then joins the results in Python.

Python

```
#  Inefficient: Multiple queries
for author in Author.objects.all():
   for book in author.book_set.all(): #  One query per author
   print(book.title)

#  Efficient: Two queries
```

```python
for author in
Author.objects.prefetch_related('book_set').all():
  for book in author.book_set.all():
  print(book.title)
```

prefetch_related('book_set') pre-fetches the books for each author, reducing the number of database queries.

- only() **and** defer(): These methods allow you to control which fields are retrieved from the database.[7]
  - only(): Retrieves only the specified fields.
  - defer(): Excludes the specified fields.

Python

```python
#  Retrieve only the name field
authors = Author.objects.only('name').all()
#  Exclude the biography field
authors = Author.objects.defer('biography').all()
```

- These are useful when you don't need all the fields of a model, reducing the amount of data transferred from the database.
- iterator(): If you're processing a large number of objects, iterator() can help reduce memory consumption. It retrieves objects in chunks, rather than loading them all into memory at once.

Python

```
for author in Author.objects.iterator():
    # Process each author
    print(author.name)
```

- **raw()**: In rare cases where the ORM cannot express the query you need, you can use raw() to execute raw SQL queries. However, use this sparingly, as it can make your code less portable and more vulnerable to SQL injection if not used carefully.

Python

```
authors = Author.objects.raw('SELECT * FROM myapp_author WHERE name = %s', ['John Doe'])
```

2. Database Indexing

Database indexes are like indexes in a book.[8] They help the database quickly locate specific rows of data.[9] Without indexes, the database might have to scan the entire table to find the data you're looking for, which can be slow for large tables.[10]

- **Automatic Indexing:** Django automatically creates an index on the primary key of each model.[11]
- **Explicit Indexing:** You should explicitly create indexes on fields that you frequently use in your queries, especially in filter() and order_by() clauses.

Python

```
from django.db import models
class Book(models.Model):
            title    =    models.CharField(max_length=200,
db_index=True) #  Create an index on the title field
            author    =    models.ForeignKey(Author,
on_delete=models.CASCADE)
  publication_date = models.DateField()
  class Meta:
    indexes = [
      models.Index(fields=['author', 'publication_date']),    #
Create a composite index
    ]
```

- o db_index=True: This field option creates an
  index on the title field.
- o indexes: The Meta option allows you to define
  more complex indexes, such as composite
  indexes (indexes on multiple fields).

3. Database Schema Design

How you structure your database schema can also
significantly impact performance.

- **Normalization:** Normalizing your database (reducing
  data redundancy) can improve data integrity and
  update performance.[12] However, it can sometimes lead
  to more complex queries that require joins, which can
  be slow.
- **Denormalization:** In some cases, denormalizing your
  database (adding some redundancy) can improve read
  performance by reducing the need for joins.[13] However,

this comes at the cost of increased complexity in data updates and potential data inconsistencies.

- **Data Types:** Choose the appropriate data types for your fields. For example, use IntegerField for integers, not CharField.
- **Foreign Keys:** Use Foreign Keys to define relationships between tables. This helps maintain data integrity and can improve query performance when used with select_related() and prefetch_related().

4. Database-Specific Tuning

PostgreSQL and MySQL have various configuration settings that can be tuned for optimal performance.[14] This is an advanced topic that often requires database administrator expertise.

Real-World Examples

- **E-commerce Website:**
  - Use select_related() and prefetch_related() to efficiently retrieve product details and related information (e.g., categories, images).
  - Create indexes on fields used for filtering and sorting products (e.g., price, category, rating).
  - Optimize database schema for product catalog and order management.
- **Social Media Platform:**
  - Use caching and denormalization to display user timelines and feeds quickly.
  - Optimize queries for retrieving user posts, comments, and followers.

- Consider using database partitioning or sharding for very large datasets.

By applying these database optimization techniques, you can ensure that your Django applications can handle large amounts of data and high traffic loads, providing a fast and responsive user experience.[15]

12.3 Security Best Practices (CSRF, XSS, SQL Injection Prevention)

Security should be a top priority throughout the development lifecycle. Neglecting security can lead to serious consequences, including data breaches, loss of user trust, and financial damage.[1]

Here are some of the most common web vulnerabilities and how Django helps you prevent them:

1. Cross-Site Request Forgery (CSRF)

- **What is it?**
    - CSRF is an attack where a malicious website, email, blog, instant message, or program causes a user's web browser to perform an unwanted action on a trusted site when the user is authenticated.[23]
    - For example, if a user is logged in to their bank's website, a malicious site could try to submit a

form to transfer money from the user's account without their knowledge.

- **How Django helps:**
  - Django has built-in CSRF protection.[4] It works by adding a hidden, unpredictable token to each form.
  - When the form is submitted, Django verifies that the token is present and valid. This prevents malicious sites from submitting forms on behalf of the user.
- **How to use it:**
  - Always use the {% csrf_token %} template tag in any form that uses the POST, PUT, PATCH, or DELETE HTTP methods.

HTML

```
<form method="post">
  {% csrf_token %}
  {#  ... form fields ... #}
  <button type="submit">Submit</button>
</form>
```

  - Django's CSRF middleware ('django.middleware.csrf.CsrfViewMiddleware') must be enabled in your MIDDLEWARE setting in settings.py. It's usually enabled by default.
- **Important Notes:**

- Never disable CSRF protection unless you have a very specific reason and understand the security implications.
- If you're building an API that's consumed by JavaScript, you might need to use techniques to include the CSRF token in your AJAX requests.

2. Cross-Site Scripting (XSS)

- **What is it?**
  - XSS attacks occur when an attacker injects malicious JavaScript code into a website.[5] This code can then be executed in the user's browser, allowing the attacker to steal cookies, hijack sessions, or modify the page content.
  - For example, if a website allows users to submit comments that are displayed on the page without proper sanitization, an attacker could include JavaScript code in a comment.[6]
- **How Django helps:**
  - Django's template engine automatically escapes HTML characters in variables.[7] This means that if you display user-provided data, any potentially dangerous HTML tags will be rendered as plain text.

HTML

```html
<p>User Comment: {{ user_comment }}</p>
```

- If user_comment contains `<script>alert('XSS');</script>`, Django will render it as:

HTML

```
<p>User Comment: &lt;script&gt;alert(&#x27;XSS&#x27;);&lt;/script&gt;</p>
```

- The browser will display the text `<script>alert('XSS');</script>` instead of executing the JavaScript code.
- **Important Notes:**
  - Be very careful when you explicitly tell Django *not* to escape HTML. Use the |safe template filter only when you are absolutely sure that the data is safe.

HTML

```
{# Use with EXTREME caution! #}
<p>{{ user_generated_html | safe }}</p>
```

- Always validate and sanitize user input on the server-side, even if you also do client-side validation.

3. SQL Injection

- **What is it?**
  - SQL injection is a code injection technique used to attack data-driven applications, in which malicious SQL statements are inserted into an entry field for execution (e.g., to dump the database contents to the attacker).[89]
  - For example, if a website dynamically constructs SQL queries based on user input without proper sanitization, an attacker could insert SQL code into an input field to modify the query and gain unauthorized access to the database.[10]
- **How Django helps:**
  - Django's ORM (Object-Relational Mapper) helps prevent SQL injection by abstracting away the need to write raw SQL queries.[11]
  - When you use the ORM's methods (e.g., filter(), get()), Django automatically escapes user-provided data, preventing it from being interpreted as SQL code.

Python

\# Safe from SQL injection

```
username = request.GET.get('username')
users = User.objects.filter(username=username)
```

- **Important Notes:**
  - Avoid using raw SQL queries (.raw()) whenever possible. If you must use them, be extremely careful to properly escape user input.

Other Security Considerations

- **Input Validation:** Always validate user input on the server-side. Don't rely solely on client-side validation, as it can be bypassed.
- **Password Hashing:** Never store passwords in plain text. Django's password field and authentication functions automatically handle password hashing using secure algorithms.
- **Secure Session Management:** Django's session framework provides built-in security features. Make sure you understand session security settings.
- **Security Headers:** Configure your web server to set security-related HTTP headers (e.g., X-Content-Type-Options, X-Frame-Options, Strict-Transport-Security) to further enhance security.
- **Regular Updates:** Keep your Django version, Python version, and all your dependencies up to date to patch security vulnerabilities.

Real-World Examples

- **E-commerce Website:**

- CSRF protection is essential to prevent attackers from forcing users to make purchases or change their account details.[12]
- XSS prevention is crucial to protect against attackers injecting malicious code into product reviews or user profiles.
- SQL injection prevention is vital to protect sensitive customer data, such as credit card information.[13]
- **Social Media Platform:**
  - CSRF protection prevents attackers from forcing users to post content or change their profile information.
  - XSS prevention is necessary to protect against attackers injecting malicious code into posts or comments.
  - SQL injection prevention safeguards user data and platform integrity.[14]

By understanding these common web vulnerabilities and following Django's security best practices, you can build more secure and reliable web applications that protect your users and your data.

12.4 Monitoring and Logging

Monitoring and logging are like the eyes and ears of your application. They provide insights into what's happening behind the scenes, allowing you to react to problems quickly and proactively improve your application.

Understanding Monitoring

Monitoring involves collecting and analyzing data about your application's performance and health.[1] This data can include:

- **Response Time:** How long it takes for your application to respond to requests.
- **Error Rates:** The frequency of errors occurring in your application.
- **Server Resource Usage:** CPU usage, memory usage, disk I/O.
- **Database Performance:** Query execution time, connection pool usage.
- **Traffic Volume:** The number of requests your application is handling.

Monitoring helps you:

- **Identify Bottlenecks:** Pinpoint areas where your application is slow or inefficient.
- **Detect Errors:** Quickly discover and diagnose errors.
- **Track Performance Trends:** Observe how your application's performance changes over time.
- **Proactively Address Issues:** Identify potential problems before they become critical.[2]
- **Understand User Behavior:** Gain insights into how users are interacting with your application.

Tools and Techniques for Monitoring

- **Server Monitoring Tools:** Tools like top, htop, vmstat, and iostat provide real-time information about server resource usage.
- **Application Performance Monitoring (APM):** APM tools like New Relic, Datadog, and Sentry provide detailed insights into your application's performance and errors.[3] They can track response times, database query times, and other metrics.[4]
- **Database Monitoring:** Database systems like PostgreSQL and MySQL have tools for monitoring query performance and resource usage.[5]
- **Django Debug Toolbar:** This is a Django package that provides useful information about your application's performance during development, such as the number of database queries and the time spent rendering templates. **(Note: Do not use this in production!)**
- **Custom Metrics:** You can also collect and track custom metrics specific to your application, such as the number of user registrations or the number of orders placed.

Understanding Logging

Logging involves recording events that occur within your application. These events can include:

- **Errors:** Exceptions and other unexpected events.
- **Warnings:** Potential problems or unusual situations.
- **Informational Messages:** Normal application behavior.
- **Debug Messages:** Detailed information for developers during debugging.

Logging helps you:

- **Troubleshoot Errors:** Trace the sequence of events that led to an error.[6]
- **Debug Issues:** Understand the state of your application at a specific point in time.
- **Audit Trail:** Maintain a record of important events.
- **Security Analysis:** Identify suspicious activity.

Using Django's Logging Framework

Django has a built-in logging framework based on Python's logging module. It provides a flexible and configurable way to manage logging in your application.

Here's a basic example of how to use Django's logging:

Python

```python
import logging
# Get a logger for the current module
logger = logging.getLogger(__name__)
def my_view(request):
    try:
        #  ... some code that might raise an exception ...
    except Exception as e:
        # Log the error
        logger.error(f"An error occurred: {e}", exc_info=True)
        #  ... handle the error ...
    logger.info("User accessed the my_view.")
    #  ... rest of the view ...
```

- logging.getLogger(__name__): This gets a logger that's specific to the current module. This is a best practice because it makes it easier to trace where log messages come from.
- logger.error(message, exc_info=True): This logs an error message. The exc_info=True argument is important; it adds traceback information to the log, which is invaluable for debugging.
- logger.info(message): This logs an informational message.

Configuring Django Logging

You configure Django's logging in the LOGGING dictionary in your settings.py file. This allows you to control:

- **Loggers:** Which parts of your application generate log messages.
- **Handlers:** Where log messages are sent (e.g., console, files, email).[7]
- **Formatters:** How log messages are formatted.
- **Levels:** The severity of log messages (e.g., DEBUG, INFO, WARNING, ERROR, CRITICAL).[8]

Here's a basic LOGGING configuration:

Python

```
LOGGING = {
    'version': 1,
    'disable_existing_loggers': False,
    'formatters': {
        'verbose': {
```

```
                'format': '{levelname} {asctime} {module}
{process:d} {thread:d} {message}',
            'style': '{',
        },
        'simple': {
            'format': '{levelname} {message}',
            'style': '{',
        },
    },
    'handlers': {
        'console': {
            'level': 'INFO',
            'formatter': 'simple',
            'class': 'logging.StreamHandler',
        },
        'file': {
            'level': 'ERROR',
            'formatter': 'verbose',
            'class': 'logging.FileHandler',
            'filename': 'error.log',
        },
    },
    'loggers': {
        'django': {
            'handlers': ['console'],
            'level': 'INFO',
            'propagate': True,
        },
        'myapp': {
            'handlers': ['console', 'file'],
            'level': 'DEBUG',
            'propagate': False,
```

```
    },
  },
}
```

- **version**: The version of the logging configuration format (always 1).
- **disable_existing_loggers**: Whether to disable Django's default loggers.
- **formatters**: Defines how log messages should be formatted.
- **handlers**: Specifies where log messages should be sent (e.g., to the console, to a file).
- **loggers**: Configures loggers for different parts of your application.

Best Practices

- **Log Levels:** Use appropriate log levels (DEBUG, INFO, WARNING, ERROR, CRITICAL) to categorize your log messages.[9]
- **Structured Logging:** Consider using structured logging (e.g., JSON) to make your logs easier to parse and analyze.
- **Log Rotation:** Implement log rotation to prevent log files from growing too large.
- **Centralized Logging:** For complex applications, consider using a centralized logging system to collect logs from multiple servers.
- **Monitoring Integration:** Integrate your logging system with your monitoring tools to correlate events and metrics.[10]

Real-World Examples

- **E-commerce Website:**
    - Monitoring: Track response times for product pages and checkout processes, monitor database query performance, and track the number of orders placed.
    - Logging: Log errors during order processing, log user authentication attempts, and log any suspicious activity.
- **Social Media Platform:**
    - Monitoring: Track the number of active users, the time it takes to load feeds, and the performance of the search functionality.
    - Logging: Log user actions (e.g., creating posts, comments, likes), log errors when processing user requests, and log any security-related events.[11]

By implementing effective monitoring and logging practices, you can gain valuable insights into your application's behavior, identify and resolve issues quickly, and ensure a smooth and reliable user experience.

12.5 Scalability Considerations

When you build a web application, you want it to be able to handle a growing number of users and requests. Scalability is the ability of your system to handle this increased load. If you don't design for scalability from the start, you might encounter performance bottlenecks, slow response times, and even system failures as your application grows.

Here are the primary approaches to scaling your Django application:

1. Vertical Scaling (Scaling Up)

- **What it is:** Vertical scaling involves increasing the resources of a single server. This means upgrading the server's CPU, RAM, storage, or network bandwidth.
- **Pros:**
  - Relatively simple to implement (in the short term).
  - Often requires minimal code changes.
- **Cons:**
  - Limited by the maximum capacity of a single server.
  - Can become expensive as you need more powerful hardware.
  - Single point of failure: If the server goes down, your entire application is unavailable.
- **Example:**
  - If your Django application is running on a server with 4GB of RAM and you start experiencing performance issues under heavy load, you could upgrade the server to 16GB of RAM.

2. Horizontal Scaling (Scaling Out)

- **What it is:** Horizontal scaling involves adding more servers to handle the load. This distributes the traffic and processing across multiple machines.

- **Pros:**
  - Can scale to handle very high traffic volumes.
  - Provides redundancy: If one server fails, others can take over.
  - More cost-effective than vertical scaling for very large applications.
- **Cons:**
  - More complex to implement.
  - Requires careful design and architecture.
  - Introduces challenges like load balancing and data synchronization.
- **Example:**
  - Instead of running your Django application on a single server, you run it on multiple servers, and a load balancer distributes incoming requests among them.

Key Scalability Techniques for Django

Here are some specific techniques and architectural patterns to consider when scaling your Django application:

- **Load Balancing:**
  - Distributes incoming traffic across multiple servers to prevent any single server from becoming overloaded.[1]
  - Tools like Nginx or HAProxy can be used as load balancers.
  - Load balancers can also perform health checks on servers and route traffic away from unhealthy instances.
- **Database Scaling:**

354

- As your data grows, your database can become a bottleneck.
- **Read Replicas:** Create read-only copies of your database to handle read-heavy operations (e.g., displaying data to users). Writes are still directed to the primary database.
- **Database Sharding:** Partition your database into smaller, independent databases (shards). Each shard handles a subset of the data. This is a complex technique but can significantly improve performance for very large datasets.
- **Database Caching:** Use caching techniques (as discussed in Chapter 12.1) to reduce the load on your database.
- **Caching:**
  - Caching is crucial for scaling. Cache frequently accessed data to reduce the number of database queries and server-side processing.
  - Use a distributed caching system like Redis or Memcached to share cached data across multiple servers.
- **Asynchronous Tasks (Celery):**
  - Offload long-running or computationally intensive tasks to a task queue.
  - Celery is a popular task queue library for Django. It allows you to run tasks asynchronously in the background, freeing up your web servers to handle user requests.
  - Examples of tasks that can be handled asynchronously: sending emails, processing images, generating reports.
- **Message Queues (RabbitMQ, Kafka):**

- For highly scalable and distributed systems, message queues like RabbitMQ or Kafka can be used to decouple different parts of your application.
  - Services communicate by sending and receiving messages through the queue.
- **Microservices Architecture:**
  - Instead of building a monolithic application, you can break it down into smaller, independent services.
  - Each microservice handles a specific function (e.g., user management, order processing).
  - Microservices can be scaled and deployed independently.
  - This is a complex architectural pattern but provides great flexibility and scalability.
- **Content Delivery Network (CDN):**
  - Use a CDN to distribute your static assets (CSS, JavaScript, images) across multiple servers around the world.
  - This reduces latency for users, as the assets are served from a server closer to them.

Real-World Examples

- **E-commerce Website:**
  - Load balancing to distribute traffic during peak shopping periods.
  - Read replicas to handle product catalog views and order history queries.
  - Caching to speed up product page loading.

- Celery to process order confirmations and shipping updates asynchronously.
- **Social Media Platform:**
  - Database sharding to handle the massive volume of user data and posts.
  - Caching to display user feeds and timelines quickly.
  - Message queues to handle real-time updates and notifications.
  - Microservices to manage user profiles, posts, and messaging.

Scalability is an ongoing process. You'll need to monitor your application's performance, identify bottlenecks, and adapt your architecture as your needs evolve. By considering these scalability techniques, you can build Django applications that are ready to handle the demands of a growing user base.

Conclusion

Congratulations! You've reached the end of "Full-Stack Django Essentials," and in doing so, you've taken a significant step toward becoming a proficient full-stack Django developer. We've covered a wide range of topics, from the foundational principles of Django's MTV architecture to the intricacies of building robust backends, crafting engaging frontends, and deploying your applications to the cloud.

Throughout this journey, we've emphasized the power and elegance of Django, a framework designed to empower developers to build complex web applications efficiently and effectively. You've learned how to:

- **Structure your applications** with Django's models, views, and templates.
- **Interact with databases** using Django's ORM.
- **Create dynamic and interactive user interfaces**.
- **Build RESTful APIs** with Django REST Framework.
- **Secure your applications** against common web vulnerabilities.
- **Optimize performance** for scalability.
- **Deploy your projects** to a production environment.

However, this book is not an endpoint. The world of web development is constantly evolving. Consider this a strong foundation upon which you can build a successful and fulfilling career.

Where to Go From Here

The skills you've acquired in this book are highly transferable, but continued learning is essential. Here are some key areas to focus on:

- **Deepen Your Django Expertise:** Explore advanced Django features like signals, middleware, and caching in greater depth. The official Django documentation remains your most valuable resource.
- **Master Frontend Technologies:** Continue to refine your HTML, CSS, and JavaScript skills. Consider exploring modern JavaScript frameworks like React or Vue.js to build even more sophisticated user interfaces.
- **Expand Your Database Knowledge:** Learn more about database optimization techniques, database administration, and potentially explore other database systems.
- **Embrace DevOps Practices:** Invest time in understanding CI/CD, containerization (Docker), and cloud computing. These skills are increasingly important in modern web development.
- **Contribute to the Community:** The Django community is vibrant and welcoming. Participate in forums, contribute to open-source projects, and share your knowledge with others.

A Final Word

Building web applications is a rewarding endeavor. You have the power to create tools that solve problems, connect people, and make a real impact. Embrace the challenges, celebrate your successes, and never stop learning.

We hope that "Full-Stack Django Essentials" has provided you with the confidence and skills to embark on this exciting journey. Now, go out there and build something amazing!

Appendix A: Django Resources and Further Learning

This appendix provides a curated collection of resources to help you deepen your Django knowledge, stay up-to-date with the latest trends, and find solutions to common problems.

Official Django Documentation

The official Django documentation is your primary source of truth. It's comprehensive, accurate, and regularly updated.

- **What it offers:**
    - Detailed explanations of all Django features.
    - Tutorials and how-to guides.
    - API reference for all Django modules and classes.
    - Release notes and upgrade instructions.
- **Why it's important:**
    - It's the most reliable and authoritative source of information.
    - It's always kept up-to-date with the latest Django releases.
- **Where to find it:**
    - Go to https://docs.djangoproject.com/en/4.2/ (replace "4.2" with the Django version you're using).

Useful Django Packages and Libraries

Django has a rich ecosystem of third-party packages that can extend its functionality and simplify common tasks. Here are a few categories and examples:

- **Django REST Framework (DRF):**
  - For building RESTful APIs.
  - Provides powerful tools for serialization, authentication, and more.
- **Django Allauth:**
  - Handles user authentication, registration, social authentication (like Google, Facebook), and account management.
- **Django Celery:**
  - For asynchronous task queues. Allows you to offload time-consuming tasks (like sending emails) to background processes.
- **Django Channels:**
  - Extends Django to handle WebSockets, enabling real-time functionality.
- **Django Debug Toolbar:**
  - A handy development tool that provides insights into query performance, template rendering, and other debugging information. (Use only in development, not production!)
- **Django-Filter:**
  - For creating dynamic filters for your data. Useful for search and filtering functionality.
- **Django-Crispy-Forms:**
  - Simplifies the process of creating beautiful and consistent form layouts.
- **Django-Storages:**

- Provides a consistent API for working with various storage backends (like Amazon S3, Google Cloud Storage) for your files.
- **How to find more:**
  - Search on the Python Package Index (PyPI) at https://pypi.org/.
  - Use keywords related to the functionality you need (e.g., "django authentication," "django file storage").
  - Check the package's documentation and popularity before using it.

Online Communities and Forums

Connecting with other Django developers is a great way to learn, get help, and stay up-to-date.

- **Django Forum:**
  - The official Django forum is a good place to ask questions and discuss Django-related topics.
  - Find it here: https://forum.djangoproject.com/
- **Stack Overflow:**
  - Stack Overflow is a popular question-and-answer website for programmers. You can find a wealth of Django questions and solutions there.
  - Use the "django" tag when asking or searching for questions.
  - Go to: https://stackoverflow.com/questions/tagged/django
- **Reddit:**

- The r/django subreddit is an active community for Django developers.
- Find it here: https://www.reddit.com/r/django/
- **Django Discord:**
  - A Discord server for real-time discussion and support.
  - Search online for "Django Discord" to find the invite link.

Troubleshooting Tips and Common Errors

Everyone runs into problems when coding. Here are some tips and common errors to watch out for:

- **Read the Error Messages:** Django's error messages are often very helpful. Pay close attention to what they say.
- **Tracebacks are Your Friend:** When you see an error, the traceback shows you the sequence of function calls that led to the error. This can help you pinpoint the source of the problem.
- **Check Your Settings:** Many problems are caused by incorrect settings in settings.py. Double-check your database configuration, installed apps, middleware, etc.
- **Look for Typos:** Typos are a common source of errors. Carefully review your code for spelling mistakes.
- **Use the Debugger:** Python's built-in debugger (pdb) can be a lifesaver. You can use it to step through your code line by line and inspect variables.
- **Search Online:** Use search engines to look for solutions to your specific error messages. Chances are, someone else has encountered the same problem.

- **Ask for Help:** Don't hesitate to ask for help in online communities like Stack Overflow or the Django Forum.

Common Errors:

- ImportError: This usually means that Python can't find a module or package. Check your INSTALLED_APPS setting and make sure you've installed any necessary packages.
- TemplateSyntaxError: This means there's an error in your template syntax. Double-check your template tags and variables.
- OperationalError: This is a database-related error. Check your database settings and make sure your database server is running.
- NoReverseMatch: This means that Django can't find a URL pattern with the given name. Check your urls.py files.

This appendix is your starting point for continued learning and support. The Django community is vast and helpful, so don't hesitate to reach out and explore!

Appendix B: Example Project Walkthrough

This appendix provides a complete example project that illustrates how to build a full-stack Django application from start to finish. It's designed to reinforce the concepts covered throughout the book and provide a practical demonstration of how the different components of Django work together.

Project Overview

We'll build a simplified version of a social media application, focusing on core features like:

- **User Authentication:** User registration, login, and logout.
- **Posts:** Creating, viewing, and listing posts.
- **Comments:** Adding comments to posts.

This project will touch on most of the key areas covered in the book:

- Django Models
- Django Views (Function-Based and Class-Based)
- Django Templates
- Django Forms
- Django URL Routing
- Django Admin Interface
- Django REST Framework (for a simple API component)
- Basic JavaScript/AJAX interaction

Project Structure

The project will be organized into Django apps:

- **users**: Handles user authentication and profiles.
- **posts**: Manages posts and comments.
- **api**: Provides a simple API for posts.

Detailed Walkthrough

Here's a breakdown of the steps and key code snippets we'll cover in this appendix:

1. **Setting up the Project:**
   - Creating the Django project and apps.
   - Configuring the database (PostgreSQL).
   - Setting up static files.
2. **User Authentication (users app):**
   - Defining a custom user registration form.
   - Creating views for user registration, login, and logout.
   - Using Django's built-in authentication views.
   - Creating templates for user authentication.
   - Securing views with @login_required.
   - Example Code Snippets:
     - users/forms.py (Custom user registration form)
     - users/views.py (Registration and login views)
     - users/templates/registration/register.html (Registration template)
3. **Posts (posts app):**
   - Defining the Post and Comment models.
   - Creating views to:
     - List all posts.

- Create a new post.
- View a single post with its comments.
- Add a comment to a post.
- Using Django Forms for post and comment creation.
- Creating templates to display posts and comments.
- Example Code Snippets:
  - posts/models.py (Post and Comment models)
  - posts/forms.py (Post and Comment forms)
  - posts/views.py (Post listing, creation, and detail views)
  - posts/templates/posts/post_list.html (Post listing template)
  - posts/templates/posts/post_detail.html (Post detail template)

4. **API (api app):**
   - Defining a serializer for the Post model.
   - Creating a simple API view to:
     - Retrieve a list of posts.
   - Using Django REST Framework's APIView and Response.
   - Configuring URLs for the API.
   - Example Code Snippets:
     - api/serializers.py (Post serializer)
     - api/views.py (Post API view)
     - api/urls.py (API URLs)

5. **Frontend Interaction:**
   - Demonstrating how to use JavaScript and AJAX to:

- Fetch posts from the API endpoint.
- Dynamically display posts on the page.
  - Example Code Snippets:
    - JavaScript code to fetch and display posts in posts/templates/posts/post_list.html
6. **Deployment (Simplified):**
   - Briefly covering essential deployment steps:
     - Setting DEBUG = False.
     - Collecting static files.
     - Basic web server configuration (e.g., using python manage.py runserver for simplicity, but noting that it's not for production).

Key Features of the Appendix

- **Complete Code:** The appendix will provide complete, working code for all the key components of the project.
- **Step-by-Step Explanation:** Each step will be explained in detail, with clear and concise language.
- **Emphasis on Best Practices:** The project will adhere to Django best practices for code organization, security, and performance.
- **Cross-Referencing:** The appendix will cross-reference relevant chapters in the book to reinforce the connection between concepts.
- **Focus on Clarity:** The primary goal is to make the example project easy to understand and follow.

This appendix will serve as an invaluable resource for readers, helping them to solidify their understanding of

Django and providing a solid foundation for building their own web applications.

www.ingramcontent.com/pod-product-compliance
Lightning Source LLC
Chambersburg PA
CBHW080548060326
40689CB00021B/4785